THE
FINANCIAL
PHYSICAL®

Why the Medical Profession Model
is Perfect for Financial Advisors

ANDREW V. TIGNANELLI
CPA, CFP®

Disclosure

The Financial Consulate is a registered investment advisor, and Drew Tignanelli is a registered advisor representative. Information presented herein is for educational purposes only and does not intend to make an offer or solicitation for the sale or purchase of any specific securities, investments, or investment strategies. Investments involve risk, and unless otherwise stated, are not guaranteed.

Readers of the information contained in this book should be aware that any action taken by the reader based on this information is taken at their own risk. This information does not address individual situations and should not be construed or viewed as any type of individual or group recommendation. Be sure to first consult with a qualified financial advisor, tax professional, and/or legal counsel before implementing any securities, investments, or investment strategies discussed.

Any performance shown for the relevant time periods is based upon observations and experiences of Drew Tignanelli. The client anecdotes, stories, and other examples are shared for illustrative purposes only and do not represent actual advice. Performance calculations herein have not been audited by any third party. Actual performance of client portfolios may differ materially due to the timing related to additional client deposits or withdrawals and the actual deployment and investment of a client portfolio, the length of time various positions are held, the client's objectives and restrictions, and fees and expenses incurred by any specific individual portfolio. **PAST PERFORMANCE IS NO GUARANTEE OF FUTURE RESULTS.**

Contents

Dedication

First and foremost, this book is dedicated to my wife, Beverly, who helped me start the company in 1984 and didn't retire until the company was firmly established. When I was about eight years old, I remember lying in the grass looking up to heaven and praying that I would find true love. Beverly is the answer to that prayer.

Next, the remarkable employees of the Financial Consulate who have, over the last fifteen years, helped build the Consulate. They are driven by a mission to work as a team dedicated to one another and to each client. Every day, they accomplish one of our core values: love, which is to nurture, protect, and cherish, without expectation.

I also want to thank my father, A. Andrew Tignanelli (Andy), who passed on in 2016. He was a remarkable man with amazing accomplishments. I am blessed to be his offspring, and I desire to honor him in this life. Even though he did not like my choice of career, he still helped me along the path I chose. My mother, Grace, was also the ultimate example of how behind every great man is a better woman.

Lastly, to the Father of all families, after whom my earthly father patterned many of his fathering skills. I wish I could introduce everyone to the Father of all fathers, but that is a decision we must all personally choose, for He rewards those who seek Him earnestly. Too often, we look for a genie in a bottle and not the Holy, awe-inspiring God of the universe.

Author's Note

I've been in the financial industry since 1979, helping clients with insurance, portfolio planning, and other elements of their wealth plan. Yet, if you ask me when I truly became a professional financial advisor, I'd tell you it wasn't until 1998—almost twenty years after I got my start in the industry.

Some might wonder how it took me twenty years, a period during which I received a degree in accounting, earned the CFP* designation, qualified for my CPA credential, and got my Series 6 and life insurance licenses, to reach professional status in my own mind. Clearly, the industry had bestowed professional status on me much earlier. In fact, after a mere two weeks of training, the first company I worked for slapped the *financial advisor* title on me and sent me out to sell investment and insurance products to clients.

But it wasn't until 1998 that I became a professional financial advisor. I was now fully independent of brokerage firms and insurance companies, could not take commissions or referral fees, was well educated, experienced through hard knocks, and was a fee-only fiduciary.

God also gave me the mission to try to help lessen the worry and burden of money management for the folks who crossed my path. His message to me was clear: He wanted me to stop communicating the love of money, which is one of the biggest destroyers of relationships, and instead focus on the riches my clients can gain through their real-life relationships and from fulfilling their emotional needs. He clearly wanted me to understand that money was nothing more than a tool to help my clients achieve true wealth in relationships.

This book is all about the journey I took to go from a salesperson to a professional financial advisor. It follows my experiences becoming a fee-only, independent advisor and National Association of Personal Financial Advisors (NAPFA) member, committed to providing comprehensive advice for my clients.

Over the decades, personal finances have become quite complicated. In this book, you will learn that, as with your personal health, you need a professional doctor to manage your financial health.

No one wants a medical doctor who is sales oriented. Likewise, the public is beginning to understand that they do not want a sales rep helping with their personal finances. Instead, a professional financial advisor should be similar to a general practitioner of medicine; they should be like a doctor of personal finance.

Like a medical doctor, these advisors should be highly educated in all areas of money management. Doctors of personal finance should be independent, experienced, credentialed, fee-only, and act as a fiduciary at all times (defined as working in your best interest and minimizing conflicts of interest—see further definition in the next chapter).

This book is a cautionary tale for you, the reader. In my experience, you will probably see parallels within your own financial planning journey—and warning signs indicating that those who guide your financial decisions may not have the right motivations, knowledge, or experience to play such a crucial role in your life.

As you'll learn from reading my experiences, the financial industry is focused on sales, not on financial health and wellness. In our industry, you could graduate college with a bachelor's degree in history or get a master's degree in psychology and then put up a shingle saying you're a financial advisor.

The financial industry's very culture fights against allowing their reps the time and resources to become doctors of finance, dedicated to their clients' financial well-being. Instead, the industry standard is to hire good salespeople.

If that's not what you'd want from your medical doctor, then why would you want that of the person who will guide your financial decisions and help you build and protect the wealth that can turn your goals into realities? Frankly, I don't think you would. You'd want a doctor who was unfettered by referral fees, commissions, and other competing interests, who had a legal obligation to work in the best interests of your health.

Likewise, you want to look for an independent, credentialed, experienced, comprehensive, fee-only fiduciary for your financial planning. I will tell you the story of how I learned this truth for myself.

Finally, I want to emphasize that this book is about *my* journey. It also highlights my passion to see the public demand professional advisors who are similar to doctors. The Financial Consulate and I were synonymous up to 2005, at which time the company began to emerge as an ongoing concern not dependent on me. Today, the Consulate has over twenty employees, each with their own life experiences, beliefs, passions, goals, and ambitions. Our thought processes and the ways we arrive at decisions may be very different, but they harmonize with the same passions and goals for fellow employees and for every client.

This book is not about the Consulate but about me—Drew Tignanelli—and my life experiences, goals, and personal passion to effect a positive change in public perception of what a professional financial advisor should be and do.

Introduction

Ask anyone to trace the exact path they took to evolve into what they've ultimately become, and you're probably going to get a convoluted route, twisting and turning through a hundred seemingly unimportant events. Our lives are filled with incidents, accidents, Divine intervention, and family history, all of which combine to push, lead, and drive us in one direction over another.

Sometimes, however, we can look at specific events from our pasts, or our ancestors' lives, and see the undeniable influence those things have had on who we've become. For me, this starts with my grandparents, James and Christine Tignanelli and Joe and Carmella Paradise, and their decisions to emigrate to the United States from Italy.

James, Christine, Joe, and Carmella came to this country in the early 1900s with virtually nothing. On my office wall today, I've got the plane, saw, and vise grip that my grandfather, James, brought from Italy—the only property he had.

But these weren't just possessions; they were tools. When paired with his skill as a stonemason, the tools enabled him to earn enough money to buy a small farm in Pennsylvania. This farm ultimately was an investment, an investment that paid dividends when my grandfather's knees gave out and he began working as a horticulturist, handling the landscaping at a large estate—a skill he'd honed on his own land before using it to earn money.

My grandfather's hard work might not have been used as effectively if it were not for the brilliant mathematical abilities of my grandmother, Christine, a woman who was never able to go to college. My grandfather could do anything with his hands, but Grandma was the money person in the family. The person who managed to save, accumulate, and strategically use money to better the personal lives of those involved. Grandpa's tools were metal; Grandma's tool was money.

Over the years of my career in finance, God has taught me that, like my grandfather's plane, saw, and vise grip, money is nothing more than a very good albeit neutral tool, one that can help us realize our dreams and focus on the power of relationships in our lives.

Why Am I Writing This Book Now?

In 2020, as I eased out of the CEO and president position at the Financial Consulate and moved into the role of chairman, I decided that one thing I wanted to do was focus on educating the broader public about what a true financial planning professional is. To do that, I knew I needed to write a book that would explore the differences between a salesperson and an independent, credentialed, comprehensive, fee-only planner with a fiduciary responsibility.

As an advisor, I learned that the foundation of all financial planning is the way my clients think about money. This determines everything they will do *with* and *for* money. But people who get financial advice also need to consider the way their *advisor* thinks about money and what they will do *for* money and *with* a client's money—because this determines the nature of the advice they provide. It will control whether that advice is well considered with the client's objectives and situation in mind, or whether it's led by commissions and rewards that the advisor will receive after selling a product or financial instrument.

In the financial industry, there are a variety of terms used to describe professional advisors. Whether they call themselves wealth managers, financial planners, advisors, or some other gimmicky, marketing-focused term, they should all be held to the same high standards. What's important is to look beyond the title and see what their experience is, what their motivations are, and what their responsibilities are.

For example, let's look at three descriptions—one for a salesperson, one for a financial professional who approaches planning like a doctor of personal finance, and one for a fiduciary:

Salesperson

One who gives financial advice with the sole objective to get clients to agree to apply for, buy, or invest in products (including insurance and annuities) from which they are compensated. Salespeople limit their advice to products and are not dedicated to your personal financial education and well-being. Thus, they don't consider the broad spectrum of comprehensive wealth advice.

Approaches Planning Like a Doctor of Personal Finance

Fee-only, independent, experienced, and credentialed advisor. Often National Association of Personal Financial Advisors (NAPFA) members, these planners don't push products that have commissions or advisor incentives. Instead, they educate themselves and their clients on *all* aspects of personal financial advice available, ultimately developing a holistic plan focused on satisfying the financial objectives of their clients.

Fiduciary

A financial advisor with a legal responsibility to work in the best interests of their clients. They *must* research and validate what they recommend to a client and work to avoid conflicts of interest, disclosing those that can't be avoided. *A true fiduciary follows standards based on decades of court case law and does not spell out a specialized definition for the words* fiduciary responsibility. *Over 90 percent of advisors **do not** adhere fully to a simple definition of fiduciary based on case law.*

It would be one thing if everyone were already aware of these differences, as well as the biases inherent in each. Instead, people routinely choose commission-based advisors with no fiduciary responsibility, ultimately paying as much or more than they could pay for what I refer to as a doctor of finance: a professional, credentialed, fee-only advisor practicing holistic, comprehensive wealth advice.

In this book, I share stories from my forty-year career in the financial industry to pull back the curtain and expose the good, the bad, and the ugly within the industry. It is my hope that through my story, you will get a better understanding of what you need to look for when selecting a financial advisor.

You may also recognize some common financial planning mistakes that you have been pushed into by advisors with the wrong priorities and education. It may be upsetting to see where you've been led astray in the past, but this book will also give you solutions to help you remedy past planning mistakes while also changing your mindset to better protect your future.

I'm also going to help you see why you should work exclusively with independent, fee-only advisors, especially those who are NAPFA certified and highly credentialed. What does that mean? It can mean having one or more of the most stringent, hard-to-get designations, including:

- CFP* (certified financial planner)
- CPA/PFS (certified public accountant specializing in personal finance)
- CFA (chartered financial analyst)

There are hundreds of designations an advisor can get, but most are as easy as a two-week course. Therefore, in my opinion, these three are the only designations I am willing to acknowledge. Be cautious if someone has credentials, but not one of the three above.

Finally, I'll close each chapter by introducing a critical psychological, planning, and investing concept for you to consider as a tool to help you better your financial planning.

Your thought processes, experiences, and biases all create the foundation of your financial decision-making process. With the right financial advisor working as your partner, you can learn to maximize accumulation with minimal sacrifice for a better overall balanced approach to growing your savings.

The right financial advisor will also help you use your funds as strategically and efficiently as possible, no matter what ups and downs the financial markets bring.

I pray that my story helps you understand why you deserve an advisor who approaches their work like a doctor of personal finance—a comprehensive personal financial professional who guides you in all areas of personal finance—who isn't paid by the companies selling the products they "prescribe" for you.

Chapter 1

My path into financial services wasn't a straight one. The middle child in an Italian family with three boys and two girls, I was a mixture of arrogant youth and good listener. I wasn't as outspoken as my brothers or my father, so I had no choice but to learn to listen.

Being a good listener was one of the catalysts that brought me to the financial industry. Finance wasn't my original plan. When I went to college, I wanted a career with glory. I wanted to be in the CIA or FBI. Researching this career choice, I discovered that an accounting degree and a military background as an officer made you a shoo-in for either agency.

After graduating college with an accounting degree, I got the application for Officer Candidate School. It should have been easy. I wanted to fly and had all the features the Air Force required—great eyesight, great health, college degree. But when I called my father, an Army Air Corps veteran, for advice, he pointed out the one thing I didn't have that the Air Force would definitely want: a blind respect for authority.

What my father actually said, in his inimitable, brusque way, was, "Boy, you're dumber than I thought you were. You almost got kicked out of college, twice, because you don't like authority."

I tried to object and explain that it was *dumb* authority I didn't respect, and he said, "Yeah, that's what you're going to get. You're going to go into the military, you're going to get a dumb general who tells you something to do, and you're going to tell him it's a dumb idea, and he's going to throw you in the brig for the rest of your military career."

As you can see, my father was not one to mince words. But he also wasn't one to shy away from the hard topics. So when he said that, as much as it hurt, I needed to listen.

What also added weight to his advice was that I knew he didn't have a bias against serving. In fact, at seventeen, my father lied about his age in order to join the military. I think he felt that the military was a great opportunity to learn skills and to get the GI Bill and eventually go to college, which he did, becoming a lawyer after taking the bar exam just once, all while working full time and being a dad of four.

Ultimately, I couldn't deny that my father was right. I didn't like authority. In college, I'd had some close calls with expulsion. I remember telling a member of the administration that she ought to be the head of a flower club, not the dean of student services for a university. I was a cocky young man, so when my father said that to me, I had to listen.

With my carefully laid plans cast aside, I suddenly had no idea what to do next. I was twenty-two with an accounting degree and no specific goals when I saw that a brokerage firm was coming to the school to interview people. It seemed like a good potential fit, since I knew a bit about finance, or, more specifically, trading.

When I was a kid, my parents would occasionally pull $1,000 together and buy some shares of stock. My father, in his wisdom, thought it would be good if we kids learned about stock investing and its benefits. So, in the mid- to late-1960s, he let each of us kids pay $5 for shares in a gold mining company he owned stock in.

We all went in for $5 each, but as the stock value dropped to about $4 per share, my siblings started to complain. My father, often saying I was the one kid who could figure out how to turn a nickel into a dime, suggested that I buy out my siblings, so I did. In the ensuing years, I enjoyed watching that stock every day I could. I would watch the price and take out the S&P 500 guide to look through all the names of the companies, fascinated by what they did and how they did it.

About six months after I'd bought out my siblings, the stock had gone up to roughly $8 per share. My father took the $32 stake I'd had and invested it in another stock. He kept doing that, and ten years later, I sold my stake for $280, after investing only $20.

This trading experience did not a financial advisor make, but it did show me that I enjoyed aspects of financial planning, so I decided to interview with the brokerage firm visiting my college.

Sadly, that company did not hire me. Nor did the next few I tried. Eventually, a friend of my father's introduced me to some people in the industry. I asked each one for a job, and the answer I got every time was a resounding no.

What the Industry Wants

By this point, you might be wondering what the problem was. Why was I, a college grad with an accounting degree and a solid 3.0 GPA, constantly being turned down by brokerage firms? The answer is that I lacked a vitally important thing: connections.

As a young man from an ethnic Italian family, I had no connections to rich people—despite the fact that my father was a lawyer and the Baltimore claims manager for Harleysville Mutual Insurance Company.

So what does my lack of wealthy friends have to do with my ability to work in a brokerage firm? Why did the companies instead hire only people who were well-connected with fairly wealthy people or from upper-class families in the community? Because the brokerage firms knew that people with those connections often have a willing pool of acquaintances, friends, and loved ones they can convince to invest.

One way I could have avoided this need for wealthy connections would have been to work in a sales position to build a proven sales record. Had I worked in a car dealership or an insurance agency as a sales associate, a brokerage firm would have hired me in a heartbeat. If I had worked for another brokerage firm and proved I could bring in clients, they would've hired me in a flash.

Brokerage firms whose salespeople work on commission want to on-board people who will bring them sales, either through a proven sales record or through connections they have personal influence over. For brokerages, banks and insurance companies, it's not about the personal wealth advisory skills of the people they hire or the passion they have for helping people with personal finance. It's about SALES.

The first firm willing to hire me was First Jersey Securities. I was really excited, but I'd never heard of this firm, so I asked my parents' stockbroker about them. That's when I was introduced to the term *boiler room*.[1] The goal of a boiler room is to cold-call dozens of strangers and talk them into buying a cheap, low-volume stock. Because the suggested stocks trade at low volumes, the price can quickly start to rise as orders are placed. Once the price increases, the "advisor" then calls some older clients to show them how the stock price is moving and tells them it's a good idea to get in on it now.

So, the new clients create an inflating stock price that encourages older existing clients to buy in, allowing the firm and its "advisors" to sell new clients out for a profit. Should the price begin to fall and older clients start losing too much money, the "advisor" brings them in on a newer, cheaper stock, and the cycle begins again.

---

1   Boiler Room Definition (investopedia.com)

Needless to say, I turned down the position with First Jersey Securities, a fact I'm eternally grateful for, especially since the company's president was eventually convicted of securities fraud.[2]

Because I turned down that boiler room sales position, I was available for the job offered to me in 1979 by a firm called IDS, Investor Diversified Services. You may think this is where I finally received a proper introduction to quality financial advising. Sadly, as you'll discover in Chapter 2, you'd be wrong.

The Sales Pitches

I was lucky enough to have a connection in the financial industry who could steer me away from companies like First Jersey Securities, the very worst of the industry. Even prestigious brokerage firms have a tainted reputation, yet every day, I see people fall into their traps. These firms try to make it a point of pride that you will work with an advisor from an age-old company who will make your dreams come true. However, as always, pride cometh before the fall. These firms provide little comprehensive advice and have no greater investment wisdom than independent, fee-only advisors do.

While it's true these large companies have long histories and persuasive commercials, the culture of these firms is about going out and bringing money into them. It's not about being great comprehensive financial advisors, which is what the public needs today.

The companies, and the people they employ, are not evil, but they are often dangerously incorrect. And while past work with wealthy families may have lent them an air of respectability, most who seek advice from their advisors don't have lawyers and accountants to act as checks and balances to brokers.

---

2   SEC v. First Jersey Securities, Inc., 890 F. Supp. 1185 (S.D.N.Y. 1995) :: Justia

Stockbrokers, who sometimes call themselves financial advisors, need only follow suitability parameters when recommending investments to a client. This suitability obligation simply states that an advisor must have a reasonable basis for believing that a suggested financial instrument or investment is appropriate for a client, based on their investing preferences, age, objectives, and financial position.[3]

For example, let's say a broker suggests a high-risk, speculative stock to an eighty-year-old retiree. In all likelihood, this would not be a suitable investment for that individual. But let's say a client calls one of these stockbrokers and says, "I want the most aggressive growth I can get. I have $50,000 to invest."

By following suitability requirements only, the broker can then make a growth investment with high commissions and a poor track record and be done with it. I have personally witnessed the level of damage this type of loose standard offers. In 2003 a client told me that his father had taken a $300,000 lump-sum pension from his company in 2000 and gave it to a stockbroker. By the time my client came to me, his father had only $80,000.

When you have an advisor who acts like a doctor of personal finance working for you, they will first ask you about your income, your overall savings, your debt, and so on. They will want a comprehensive picture of your overall financial health to ensure that the plan for your money is suited to your actual risk tolerance. They will act as a fiduciary, and a fiduciary must avoid conflicts of interest and have reasonable research to justify their investment suggestions.

One of the most concerning elements of the suitability obligation is that it only requires an advisor to "have a firm understanding of both the product and the customer." At no point does it require the advisor to minimize conflicts of interest, such as sales incentives, or to research

---

3   https://www.finra.org/rules-guidance/key-topics/suitability

the investment and have sound justification for why this mutual fund or stock was chosen.

Imagine if the medical profession operated this way. A doctor might prescribe a medication based solely on the patient's complaint, without checking what other medications they were taking and whether there was any potential for negative drug interactions. The doctor would look no further into the patient's request to see if maybe another drug or treatment option would be a better fit and whether the problem was more nuanced than the patient realized. You should not accept that from your physician, nor should you accept it from your financial advisor.

We all need comprehensive financial advice given by those who can analyze any situation, including taxes, estate planning, and insurance, while also providing checks and balances to investment managers, insurance agents, and others.

Unfortunately, we're not going to change the financial industry's culture overnight, which is why you can't be dazzled by the big-name company behind your broker. Instead, you need to seek out advisors who will reduce their conflicts of interest and have the training, experience, and certifications that prove their mastery over the topic of finance.

To protect yourself, make sure your advisor is independent, has valid credentials, doesn't take commissions, and is required to always be a fiduciary, with their chief compliance officer signing off on a fiduciary obligation.

Exploring Your Advisor's Biases

The commissions-based people who give you financial advice, no matter how well-meaning, have economic biases that can influence the suggestions they give, something I learned in my first fifteen years in this industry while being commission oriented. A great financial advisor will be aware of their biases and will operate under a fiduciary obligation to disclose them to you. But salespeople have no such obligation.

Can a broker, insurance agent, or bank advisor be a great financial advisor? The answer is both yes and no. Yes, if they become independent; no, if they stay in the culture of the brokerage, insurance, and bank companies that continually make profit king.

The sole objective of a salesperson is to get you to agree to buy or invest in the products they offer. This doesn't mean the products are always bad or that they won't work. Sometimes, the products offered are perfectly fine and helpful.

Yet the odds of them being the absolute best strategic option for you and your financial plan is questionable, because a salesperson does not have comprehensive knowledge of all the different selections you could make with your money and is not totally dedicated to your education and well-being.

Worse, biases in others are not always easy to understand. For example, an insurance agent might have an economic bias to undersell insurance rather than oversell. A real estate agent may have an economic bias to encourage you to take a lower offer on a home. A lawyer's bias may be to spend as little time as possible on your document preparation.

When you work with an independent, fee-only financial advisor, not only must they disclose their economic biases to you, but they can also act as a shield between you and financial salespeople who have no obligation to disclose their bias. It's like having a primary care physician explain the pros and cons of multiple treatment options, rather than simply prescribing whichever one gives them the biggest kickback.

Measuring an Advisor's Commitment

Your financial plan isn't some throwaway dream. It's a critical part of your life, your family, and your legacy. It's a commitment you're making to yourself, your community, your charitable causes, and your loved ones.

The plan may be a means to an end, but that "end" dictates the final impact your life will have. Ideally, you want to partner with an advisor who is just as committed as you are to ensuring your financial plan supports your values and goals and grants you the financial freedom to focus on the things that matter most .

If you take away one thing from this chapter, let it be this: **You're not going to get that level of commitment or expertise from a salesperson.** You need an independent advisor with a comprehensive understanding of income taxes, estate planning, insurance, mortgages, college, elder law, charitable giving, and more. You need an educated, experienced, credentialed advisor who acts as a general practitioner of personal finance, educating you to achieve a thoroughly designed wealth plan.

In other words, you need an advisor who approaches planning like a doctor of personal finance. Doctors of personal finance work on a salaried basis, not relying on the industry standard of "eating what you kill."

Tools for Financial Planning

All physicians have tools—tools that help diagnose physical ailments, identify diseases and injuries, and heal the patients they treat.

In finance, our number one tool is knowledge. In this book, I'm concentrating on knowledge in three areas:

- Financial planning
- Investing
- Financial psychology

In this chapter, I specifically want to talk about:

- The foundation of all financial planning
- Four tools for developing a financial plan
- Fear and greed

The Foundation of All Financial Planning

The way you think about money will determine everything you are going to do *with* and *for* money.

That means that no matter how much great economic advice you get, if your thinking is off-kilter and you're not willing to listen to people who can help you understand how your thinking might be off, you're going to continue to make mistake after mistake. I've seen countless examples of this throughout my career.

I've seen clients who are so fearful of taxes that they think the IRS is going to bludgeon them for anything and everything, leaving them unwilling to make any attempt to minimize their tax liability. Even going so far as not to take legitimate deductions on returns because they're so fearful.

I've met people who grew up with frugal parents who wouldn't spare a dime to allow them to buy a treat, so when they get older, they vow to never deprive themselves of anything. Next thing you know, they've spent everything they have because whenever they want something, they buy it. Still others who grew up in the same environment take it to the opposite extreme, becoming overly frugal themselves and adopting the hoarding principles of their parents.

Then there are those who think that money's powerful and will be the solution to all their problems, so they make the pursuit of money their priority. In turn, they destroy the only thing that holds any real power—relationships.

As you'll learn in the coming chapters, I've also confronted my own financial demons and lived to retrain my brain around money, ultimately saving my marriage.

The way you think about money is far more important than anything else you do. There are plenty of great investors out there, but why only one Warren Buffett? Because Buffett's mentality is perfectly aligned with being an investor. He quickly understands what a sound company looks like, and he is not prone to worry about negative things. He is not eager in his pursuit of money, but seems far more delighted by the process of investing itself. Lastly, he's always been an optimist, and as Charles Schwab famously said in his book, *Invested*, "An investor must always be an optimist."[4]

Four Tools for Developing a Financial Plan

If there's one thing my grandfather knew when he emigrated from Italy, it's that you need to have the right tools for the job. While a plane, saw, and vise grip were the right devices for his work, a financial plan, whether it's focused on retirement or just general financial wellbeing, requires a different set of tools.

Goals

The first tool is simple: know your goals. That means having specific objectives for your life over a variety of time periods. Goals, not age, should determine how you invest. What are you trying to accomplish in a week, a month, a year, five years, ten years, or thirty years? If you set

---

4   https://www.foxbusiness.com/markets/charles-schwab-successful-investor-optimist

goals, you'll get there. If you don't, you'll get somewhere—you just have no idea where that's going to be.

Also, if you are married, it is best to set your lifelong financial goals with your spouse. (I've witnessed some awkward husband-and-wife interactions when I've asked about financial goals.) To open the subject, go to dinner and look your spouse in the eye and say, "Honey, what are *your* financial goals for us? What do you think our financial priorities should be?"

Risks

The next tool is an assessment of the amount of risk you are willing to accept to accomplish each goal. This starts, as you might have guessed, with thinking about your investment risk.

Are you willing to be a pure growth investor? Are you willing to go more aggressively into individual stocks instead of a good, diversified pool of a mutual fund or index fund? Are you willing to start a business? Are you going to use leverage?

These are all levels of risk that you're bringing into the equation. Your goals should determine your risk profile, along with your psychological makeup and willingness to accept volatility. But remember, volatility is required if you're going to make a good rate of return. If your principal doesn't fluctuate a lot in value, you are not going to make a good rate of return.

But there's more to risk than investment risk. There is the risk of dying early, becoming disabled and unable to work, having an auto accident with an uninsured driver, your home burning down—the list goes on. Your question about each of these risks is twofold: "Will I be able to handle it? How can I mitigate it?" You can't insure and protect against every risk, so you have to think out risks accordingly. What risks are you willing to accept, and what risks are you willing to diversify or insure away?

While you can't insure against every risk, you can insure against losses brought on by some. Still, you only have so much money to spend on insurance, so you need to make sure you use it wisely. For many, this process starts with getting an insurance agent, but this is a mistake.

Insurance agents sell insurance; they do not do risk management. When it comes to home and auto insurance, few agents consider your other assets, your net worth, and your income when helping you secure coverage and determine a deductible. And because there is no financial interest for them, few have any interest in doing more than keeping you at whatever insurance level you're at when you first apply (this is explained in greater detail in Chapter 8).

On the other end of the spectrum, you have life insurance agents who can increase their commissions by selling you more death benefit—whether you need it or not. Since their commissions also increase based on the policy types they sell you, they tend to focus very narrowly on the insurance policy that most benefits them, rather than considering your risks and true need for the insurance.

For true risk mitigation, I believe it's vital to include an independent, fee-only, experienced, trained, educated insurance advisor to your risk management planning.

Balance Sheet

Our third tool is your balance sheet. This is a document that shows you exactly what assets and liabilities you have at any one time. It offers a bird's-eye view that helps planners better analyze the individual benefits and drawbacks of your various debts, accounts, and investments. It can quickly show us what's working to help you reach your goals and what's getting in the way.

It also shows the relationship between your cost of assets to return on assets. Too often people hold debt that is costly for some psychological benefit or hold low-yielding assets due to emotionally motivated decisions.

Cash Flow Analysis

A cash flow analysis is a breakdown of *all* your income and spending over an annual basis, and it's probably the **BEST TOOL** for all your financial planning.

The cash flow analysis essentially tells you where your money is coming in from and where it is going out on a daily, weekly, monthly, yearly, and decade-long term. This is a critical part of planning, and yet very few people actually look at cash flow on a regular basis.

To underscore its importance, let's consider what the cash flow analysis does for you. First, it allows you to see where your money's coming in, which immediately tells you the risk associated with your income. For example, if the majority of your money comes from your employer, you then know that your income is going to disappear if something ever happens to them or if you can no longer work for them due to an illness or disability.

Next up is your spending. For many, a prework coffee from a coffee shop might seem like a forgettable expense, but at $3.50 a pop over five days per week, this amounts to $910 per year. Seeing this expense on a cash flow analysis gives you the opportunity to evaluate whether you really want to be spending almost $1,000 per year on coffee, or whether that doesn't meet your financial priorities. If your goal is to retire in ten years and you're only saving $5,000 a year, you may decide that homemade coffee is a better way to go.

Your day-to-day spending impacts all your future goals, so the cash flow analysis is crucial for finding problem spending and then setting a budget. It forces you to account for all your spending, so you no longer wonder where your income is going. Then, you can change your spending and saving habits.

What we basically want is for everyone to pay themselves first, a phrase you've probably heard before because it is always a great principle. This can be as simple as putting an extra $200 a month into your 401(k). Often, when clients do this, they're absolutely astonished that they can put away $200 more a month and still be quite content with what they've bought during the month. The cash flow analysis helps us understand whether we can implement that strategy, or whether the client is overspending and possibly increasing debt on wasteful expenses.

Let's take a moment to put the concept of wasteful expenses into perspective. This can be especially difficult when we go back to the foundation of all financial planning being that the way you think about money determines what you do *with* and *for* money. To start, I will talk about my own experiences discovering and changing wasteful spending through cash flow analysis.

In 1992, I used to go out to lunch every day. We'd go down to a little pizza parlor and get a sub or pizza, or we'd get a salad from the grocery store next door. When I did my first cash flow analysis, I found that by the end of the year, I'd spent about $1,200 on lunch. Now, $1,200 a year wasn't the end of the world, but it was a fair amount of money.

Thinking back, I realized that as a kid, my school lunches had been a pretty dismal affair. Prepared the night before by my mom, these paper-sack meals of bologna on bread often wilted in the locker at my non-air-conditioned school for hours before I ate them. Already not a fan of bologna, I disliked it even more when it tasted more like what you'd expect from a sandwich slowly roasting in a hot locker for hours.

Fridays were different. On Fridays, my father would give each of us kids a quarter to buy a hot lunch of milk and a hamburger. It was heaven. I couldn't wait for Fridays. To me, that hot lunch was the best. When I got older, I held on to that mentality that bringing lunch from home was no fun and, in fact, would taste strange, and instead decided to have "hot lunch" every day. Once I did the cash flow analysis, however, I realized how much money this decision was costing me.

Now, I'm a reasonably good cook, and I enjoy cooking, so on the weekends I often prepare large meals and then put the extra in the refrigerator. Since my wife doesn't like leftovers and I do, I realized I could simply take these leftovers to work and have great lunches at a fraction of the cost. This also meant less food waste. Just like that, I was saving about $1,200 per year and not suffering in the least.

The switch to a packed lunch was an easy decision, as I enjoy my cooking and it didn't hurt my quality of life. But not all spending adjustments are that simple and straightforward. If you're struggling to decide what expenses to give up or minimize, remember that while you can't spend everything as if only today exists, you also can't save everything for tomorrow. You need to live today for today and save for tomorrow, knowing it's going to show up.

If you're depriving your family and yourself of everything because you're saving for the future—that's no better than spending everything as if tomorrow is never going to come. You can't live just for today, and you can't live just for tomorrow. Enjoy today and be ready for tomorrow when it arrives.

Fear and Greed: The Evil Empire of the Investor

When financial advisors have a sales focus, they often get commissions by playing off the one battle that all investors and savers face: the battle between greed and fear. While fear and greed may be helpful instincts in other areas of life, they will annihilate the possibility of investing success.

Earlier in this chapter, I shared with you the Charles Schwab quote, "An investor is always an optimist." One of the best examples of optimism without greed in investing is Warren Buffett. Buffett didn't start investing so that he could become the richest man on earth one day. He simply loved numbers and data and coming up with ideas that made money for himself and his investors.

A collector from childhood, Buffett progressed from stamps, coins, and bottle caps into stocks.[5] An eternal optimist, there is no fear in Buffett, at least as it relates to investing.[6] The foundation of this optimism is his wholehearted belief that the USA and other developed countries are the greatest markets and industries and that they will dominate and continue to grow the world's economy better than any other sector.[7]

Omaha residents who, for decades, have watched Buffett drive one of his used Cadillacs to McDonald's or from work back to the modest home he bought for $31,500 in 1958 would likely be the first to point out his lack of greed.[8]

There may only be one Warren Buffett, but any good investor can mirror his outlook, his patience, and his humility to help overthrow the fear and greed that threaten to infiltrate investing decisions. But optimism doesn't come naturally to some people. Thus, it's not unusual to meet clients who see the market at a high point and think it's bound to go down, just like it did in 2008.

And maybe they're right—it will go down. But, as it did in 2008, it will also rise again. A properly structured plan protects you from fear, but it also prevents you from making decisions based on greed. When

5   The Snowball: Warren Buffett and the Business of Life, by Alice Schroeder

6   https://www.kiplinger.com/article/investing/t047-c032-s014-warren-buffett-s-famous-saying-bears-repeating-now.html

7   https://www.reuters.com/article/us-buffett-forbes/buffett-calls-pessimists-about-united-states-out-of-their-mind-idUSKCN1BV0A3

8   https://www.businessinsider.com/warren-buffett-modest-home-bought-31500-looks-2017-6

you invest, it should never be because you think a certain investment is going to make you a ton of money. Instead, you should always go in thinking that it is a solid company, a logical choice that's doing well and the price is more than reasonable based on its prospects.

If you're not thinking about stocks from a logical point of view, you're in serious trouble.

Ultimately, your portfolio can easily handle another 2008 if it's structured properly for your goals and objectives. If your financial advisor tells you that their goal is to help you sell at the top and buy at the bottom, then they are fooling themselves, because no advisor can do that. Not Buffett or anyone.

Rather, push for your goals and objectives to lead your portfolio's design so that you have secured funds to help you through market volatility without affecting your long-term needs and goals.[9]

---

9   For more information about these topics and more, please visit the Financial Consulate's Knowledge Center:
https://financialconsulate.com/knowledge-center/

Chapter 2

By August 1979, it was finally happening. I was about to embark on my professional career. All I had to do was go to Minneapolis for a training course—one that lasted all of two weeks.

If two weeks doesn't sound to you like enough time to learn how to help people with their financial plan, you're right. During that short time, we learned what the firm thought was most important: how to do cold calls, how to prospect for clients, and how to get a client to say yes. That was it. I don't think we ever talked about investing options or true diversification—even mutual funds were hardly discussed. Essentially, what I got was a two-week vacation in Minneapolis learning how to be a salesperson.

It wasn't for lack of time that important investing and financial planning principles were skipped. Each day of the two-week training, we had meetings only from about 9 a.m. until 2 p.m. After that, we went out to dinner, had drinks, and networked. The reason there was no focus on anything other than selling was that the company was only focused on sales—this is how the industry was in 1979 and **still is today.**

Entering a Sales-Focused Industry

A sales-focused approach to training is still being employed by 90 percent of the industry. Even in 2022, companies like this continue to hire people, give them no training or experience on how to be an advisor, and throw them out on the street to give financial guidance to you! The fallout of this negligent training is not just that people like you get uninformed, biased financial advice; it also means that these firms have a great deal of advisor turnover. Some firms know that they will lose a large number of their poorly trained salespeople, and yet, they do nothing to change this. Why? Because these firms know that each of these advisors, before they quit, will bring in one or more new clients. When they leave, those clients they brought in will be turned over to more successful salespeople.

Are these firms recruiting advisors, or is this just another method for getting clients? They've created a revolving door of salespeople, and they don't care because at the end of the day, each salesperson who brings in one or two new clients increases revenue. And maybe they also find a few sales princes in the process, which more than compensates for the frogs.

There is a famous scene in the stage play and movie *Glengarry Glen Ross* when the sales trainer, Blake, brags about his material success as a means of motivating his trainees. This scene came to life for me while I was at IDS while working with a man named Quentin.

The quintessential salesman, Quentin managed our office. Like Blake in *Glengarry Glen Ross*, Quentin would give motivational talks and brag about living in a mansion in the richest county of the country, having Farrah Fawcett as a neighbor, and point out that his Mercedes was the most expensive car in the parking lot. Everything about Quentin was sales. His focus, even when giving you a lesson in how to shake hands with a person, was always on manipulation, and that stuff just drove me crazy.

I'll never forget Quentin's tie clip. It had a number engraved on it, and he'd ask you if you knew what that number meant. Then he'd say,

"That's the most money any American typically has when they retire at sixty-five years of age. And you're gonna make a difference in that, son. You're gonna make sure they have hundreds of thousands of dollars!"

That is the lure of sales, and it's a lure that attracts salespeople and clients alike. It's the lure of astronomical accumulation and commissions, simply by selling an investment or insurance product. The lure is shiny, but it misses the point of actual financial planning. It pays no attention to risk mitigation, cash flow, or planning that revolves around an individual's ultimate goals.

This is one of the reasons I feel so strongly about suggesting advisors who are credentialed. When you have earned the Certified Financial Planner (CFP®) designation, the Certified Public Accountant with Personal Financial Specialist (CPA/PFS) license, or the Chartered Financial Analyst (CFA) designation, you show that you're dedicated to education and professional standards. Only when they have a professional credential, education, experience, are fee-only, and are a fiduciary should anyone be able to call themselves financial advisors, financial planners, or financial consultants.

Once again, let me bring in the example of a medical professional. Would you want your general practitioner to begin treating you after they have a couple of weeks' training conducted by a single drug company? Of course not! You want your GP to have gone through years of education, board licensing, and residency. You also want them to be familiar with treatments and pharmaceuticals offered by a broad selection of manufacturers. They should have no bias when recommending your treatment. Why wouldn't you want the same from your financial advisor?

It is my hope that one day, the United States will regulate financial advisors like they do CPAs and lawyers, and that requirements will be established for them to be educated, experienced, fee-only, independent, credentialed, and held to a complete fiduciary standard

before they are permitted to tell people they are an advisor. That hasn't happened yet, which means it's completely up to you to understand what you want out of a financial advisor and to find one who provides services like a doctor of personal finance.

On My Own

After the brief training, IDS pushed me out of the nest and into the sales pit where I quickly became one of the better salespeople in the country. The secret to my success wasn't so much about what I was doing as it was what the stock market was doing.

At that time, interest rates were rising while the market was falling. All I had to do to secure my success was to go see orphaned IDS clients, whose former advisors had left the company. These neglected folks generally had mutual funds they'd owned for fifteen years that were worth the same amount they had initially put in over a decade before. I simply met with each of these clients and suggested the IDS fixed annuity, which had a yield of about 8 or 9 percent at that time, far outperforming their mutual funds.

The annuity contracts I sold were not bad products for the clients, but each of these people would likely have been better off with a more comprehensive approach to planning. Because while the annuity rate rose as interest rates did, the peak hit in about 1981. After that, the stock market went up tenfold in the next twenty years.[10]

A true financial advisor might have had these clients put some money in the annuity and also suggested they invest in stocks, review their insurance policies, and discuss their estate planning needs. But that wasn't my job. As a salesperson, my job was to make the client say yes. At this time in my life, I was the furthest thing from a professional financial advisor.

---

10 https://www.google.com/finance/quote/.DJI:INDEXDJX?sa=X&ved=2ahUKEwil-0vm77uz3AhXSZTABHbXJAhkQ3ecFegQIHRAg&window=MAX

Despite taking a less than comprehensive approach to financial planning, my clients saw me as a hero—and so did IDS. All I had to do was find orphan clients with lots of old money stuck doing nothing and sell them the IDS fixed annuity with a high interest rate. It went on this way for about four months before my then-manager, Jake, told me he was leaving and forming his own company.

The big reason behind his decision was that the contract we had with IDS included a clause that prevented us from taking our clients with us to a new brokerage. So the longer we stayed and the larger we built our client list, the more clients we'd have to leave behind with IDS.

This is another great example of the methods used by some banks and brokerages to keep clients. Not only are agents given a large, up-front commission on the sale of an annuity, but they are often paid a trailing commission for years after the sale, so a single client with one annuity can equal many years' worth of commissions. The agent agreement with IDS, however, specified that when leaving the firm, you could not take your clients with you, which means no opportunities to sell them additional, and often better or more suitable, products once you leave. This was why Jake was so keen on leaving. So when he created his own broker-dealer, I joined him.

Now, however, a new problem arose. Without the IDS annuity to sell to clients and without the IDS list of orphaned clients to pick from, it became a lot more difficult to find clients, and my sales suffered. Help soon came, though, through a very unlikely source: my father.

Pro versus Pro

My father was a salaried worker his entire life, and my brothers followed his lead. Dad's philosophy was that you go to work for one company, you dedicate yourself to them, and they'll take care of you all your life. This wasn't uncommon, or untrue, for many workers in the 1950s and 1960s, but by this time—1980—pensions were breathing their last in the public sector, and the new 401(k) profit-sharing plan was taking hold, leaving workers to scramble for their own retirement plans.[11]

Still, my father wasn't fond of the idea of working in a commission-based profession. Despite our ideological differences, he wanted to help me and ended up doing so through structured settlements. A structured settlement is essentially a periodic payment of a lawsuit settlement, often funded through annuities. As senior vice president of claims for an insurance company, my father had heard of structured settlements and realized that they might be something the insurance company needed to use. So he suggested I find out about them and said that if his company ever wanted to do one, they'd pass it through me.

I was excited by this possibility and began researching. Roughly one month later, I placed my very first structured settlement, a $400,000 case, with National Indemnity, a subsidiary of Berkshire Hathaway. At that time, Ajit Jain was the head of the insurance division where I placed the case. Today, you might be more familiar with Ajit in his role as Berkshire Hathaway's vice chairman of insurance operations.[12]

Back when I brought him my first structured settlement, he was simply a brilliant underwriter. Since that time, Jain has basically developed and scaled the underwriting concepts of Berkshire Hathaway as it grew. In many of his shareholder meetings, Buffett has extolled Jain's virtues and once described Jain as, "One of the best minds in the world."[13] But at that time, he was running the division that sold structured settlement annuities.

---

11 https://www.cnbc.com/2021/03/24/how-401k-brought-about-the-death-of-pensions.html

12 https://en.wikipedia.org/wiki/Ajit_Jain

13 https://www.cnbctv18.com/business/buffett-heaps-praise-on-ajit-jain-if-youve-got-another-son-like-this-send-him-over-5838241.htm

After that case, my father's company gave me about $3 million to $5 million worth of structured settlements each year. At the same time, I developed clients to sell financial products by doing seminars and speaking engagements. While I was focused on selling mutual funds, insurance policies, annuities, and doing structured settlements, Jake had taken a different route. Attracted to the potential for higher commissions, Jake focused on selling riskier, more niche products such as real estate limited partnerships, which were only a few years away from collapsing, or gold or diamonds, which peaked in 1980. I wasn't convinced that these investments were good fits for my clients, so I didn't sell them.

Jake was clearly focused on making money. While I certainly wasn't working for free, money wasn't my goal. I wanted to make a good living, sure, but I wanted to do so by being good at my profession, not just by being able to talk people into signing up for this or that product.

My clients likely appreciated my professional ethics, but my family was a different story. Surrounded by brothers who were salaried professionals like my father, I took some flak for having a career that they considered strictly sales. One day, my brothers, one a CPA and one a lawyer, let me know exactly how they saw my choice of career. We were attending a family gathering and the topic of investing and precious gems came up, and as I contributed to the conversation, my brothers began ripping my career to pieces, telling me that I'd become nothing more than a salesman.

It hurt. Especially since I did have higher professional ethics than some. Yet, in the back of my mind, I couldn't help thinking about Jake's focus on selling, and I started to wonder... were my brothers right? Was I on the right track?

All in all, it was a tumultuous time for me both personally and professionally, but God was there to help out with both.

Navigating Personal Loss

My faith had proven to be a priceless asset for a very long time. I mark the start of my true spiritual journey when I was a young man of fifteen and I lost my youngest sister to Reye's syndrome, essentially a swelling of the brain. It began benignly enough—she'd suffered an average case of the flu, and my parents provided the standard treatment back then, giving her chewable aspirin to break the fever. This was years before the CDC began recommending parents avoid giving children aspirin.[14]

Reye's syndrome works quickly, and within a week, despite taking her to Johns Hopkins for treatment, my sister had passed away. This devastated my parents, and in their emotional turmoil, they had little support to offer me or my siblings. Thankfully, God became an even larger presence in my life and began speaking to me during that period. In addition to setting me onto my spiritual path, He used this time to teach me to listen to the wisdom around me, a skill that has always served me.

In 1980, not only did I have a relatively new career at a new company with a spotty income, my personal life was suffering. What should have been an exciting time was instead fraught with insecurity, and I began sliding into depression. To deal with my mental state, I read books like *Johnathon Livingston Seagull,* a book about a seagull who isn't content with the average daily life and flight skills of seagulls. Instead, he seeks to learn how to master flying, eventually going from outcast to leader. The book's author, Richard Bach, has also been credited with the famous quote, "If you love something, set it free. If it comes back, it's yours. If it doesn't, it never was."[15]

I decided to apply this quote to my life and break up with my girl-friend. After all, I thought, if this was the future Mrs. Tignanelli, I should

---

14 https://www.cdc.gov/mmwr/preview/mmwrhtml/00001108.htm
15 https://www.goodreads.com/quotes/574192-if-you-love-something-set-it-free-if-it-comes

let her go and wait for her to come back and know for sure that she is the one. The breakup seemed to both surprise and devastate her, but she took that opportunity and never came back. In hindsight, it was a great blessing.

Confused and depressed, I searched for a way out. My mother came to my rescue by giving me the book, *How to Live Like a King's Kid* by former president of Curtis Engine, Harold Hill.[16] The book was about how Hill's faith drove his life. In that book, I relearned the concept that God wanted to have a relationship with me. Thinking back to when I'd lost my sister and how God had been such a comfort to me, my faith really started to grow.

During this time, my mother gave me a Bible. I sort of played Bible roulette, opening the book to a random page and seeing what passage was there. I happened to pick 1 Corinthians, chapter 13, which reads:[17]

> *If I speak with the tongues of men and of angels, but do not have love, I have become a noisy gong or a clanging cymbal. If I have the gift of prophecy, and know all mysteries and all knowledge; and if I have all faith, so as to remove mountains, but do not have love, I am nothing. And if I give all my possessions to feed the poor, and if I surrender my body to be burned, but do not have love, it profits me nothing. Love is patient, love is kind and is not jealous; love does not brag and is not arrogant, does not act unbecomingly; it does not seek its own, is not provoked, does not take into account a wrong suffered, does not rejoice in unrighteousness, but rejoices with the truth; bears all things, believes all things, hopes all things, endures all things.*

As I read this definitive description of love, I thought about my relationship with my former girlfriend. Of all the traits described in

---

16 https://openlibrary.org/books/OL5442767M/How_to_live_like_a_king%27s_kid
17 https://www.bible.com/bible/compare/1CO.13.1-7

Corinthians, I could only find two that were true of my relationship with her. In all the others, I failed. I had been jealous about everything. I had boasted about my relationship with her. I was not necessarily patient, but I was kind. I always kept a record of wrong.

As I worked through the list and began to see the truth, it became clear to me that what I'd had with her wasn't really love, which explained why the relationship hadn't lasted. I was ready to begin looking forward to whatever God had in store for me.

Our Enemy, Greed

Fissures were deepening in my relationship with Jake. He wanted to hire a new representative, Kathy, a woman he had known at another company. He sent me down to interview Kathy, and we had a productive meeting. During our lunch, she acted the part of matchmaker and set me up with a coworker of hers named Beverly—a move that turned out to be life-changing for me, though not so much for Kathy.

One week after interviewing the new representative (and matchmaker), I had my first date with my future wife, Bev. She was easy to talk to, and we had a lot in common. She also had a lot to say about our matchmaker and her working with Jake. Throughout our date, Bev opened my eyes more and more to the type of person Jake was. As Bev pulled the curtains back on who he might be, I began to see him as someone I didn't want to be associated with.

Something inside my brain clicked, and I suddenly began to see his focus on selling diamonds and limited partnerships for what it was—a greed-based way to earn the highest commissions possible. Already his focus on making more money and getting the nicest car were wearing on me. Now, motivated by Bev's description, I began a three-month crusade to figure out how to get away from him.

Moving On

While I worked to distance myself from Jake, I was drawn closer and closer to Bev. I had learned a lot about myself and relationships, and when I applied those lessons to my growing connection with Bev and looked to Corinthians to help me evaluate my relationship, I found that I was a far better person when I was with her. There was something amazing between us, and I was excited to see where it would lead.

While my business association with Jake was obviously strained, it did have some valuable moments. Not only had he motivated me to leave IDS, but he also introduced me to the Financial Planning Association, which is where I met Daniel. Daniel was a nice guy who'd been in the business for a long time. He had a basic understanding of financial planning, as much as you could within an industry that actively disdained general comprehensive knowledge. The thing that stood out about him was that he was just a nice guy trying to do reasonably good things for his clients. He was a salesman, but he wasn't focused only on how much money he could make.

Daniel never oversold or sold junk to clients, selling open-end mutual funds that allowed buyers to liquidate whenever they needed to, and cheap term insurance policies that had lower commissions, but were a very affordable, appropriate solution for most clients. Daniel was with a division of Raymond James & Associates called IM&R, Investment Management & Research.

In 1981, ready to immerse myself in a client-focused environment, I left Jake and joined Daniel who was licensed for securities with IM&R.

Daniel was a great guy to work under. His ethics, principles, and values were straightforward, and he provided the stability I needed to progress in my career. I already had an accounting degree, but Daniel encouraged me to get my Certified Financial Planner (CFP®) credential, which I did in 1981 as one of the first 5,000 people to do so.

During this time, I also gained the financial stability to start a family, which I did when I married Bev and became stepfather to her two children in 1982.

By 1983, I began wondering if I should go a step further and get my certified public accountant (CPA) credential. A friend who was a CFP* and CPA said I absolutely should. He said it helped him get more respect when talking to lawyers and accountants.

Becoming a CPA brought in a whole new air of professionalism to my career. By the end of 1984, like one of my brothers before me, I now had earned the right to put those three letters at the end of my name. Yet, I couldn't put them on my business card. I was able to tell colleagues and others I was a CPA, but at that time, professionals who earned commissions could not use the credential on their business cards, a rule that didn't change until 1991. Still, even if I couldn't update my business cards, I finally felt like I had made strides to be a professional.

Another change I made in 1984 was to become the president of the Baltimore Financial Planning Association. By this time, with defined benefit pensions becoming a rarity and 401(k) profit-sharing retirement plans taking over, thus shifting the burden of retirement savings and accumulation to the preretiree, personal finances were becoming more complex.

Tools for Financial Planning

In this chapter, I talk about a time in my career when I was both growing substantially and beginning to see the damaging impact of a sales-focused career in finance. Some of the tools I now want to share with you involve:

- Learning to appreciate the power of relationships
- Recognizing how tax prep differs from tax advice
- Feeling better about volatility

Appreciating the Power of Relationships

One of the biggest lessons that Jake missed in his focus on high commissions is that money itself is not powerful. Relationships are powerful. Money is one of the top factors in most divorces.[18] It's a relationship killer.

One of evil's classic moves is to put something in front of us that gives us a false image of what we think we want and what we think will be beneficial to us—and the love of money is one of those falsehoods. The desire for it is a beautiful, poisonous fruit that will destroy the thing that we really want, which is *relationships*.

I experienced this lesson firsthand with my wife. As a financial advisor, money is part of my every day. Not the love of money, but the study of money and associated tools and, as a result, the earning of it. Eventually, as mentioned in the last chapter, I began tracking our cash flow, down to the penny. I put us on a budget and found that every month, my wife would overspend our budget by using a credit card. And occasionally, we would fight over the credit card bill.

One day I began praying that my wife would become more financially prudent, and it struck me that in praying this way, I was framing her as the problem. Yet... what if *I* was really the problem? As I reviewed my behavior and focus over the years, I realized that I had been communicating a message to her that I loved money more than her. My actions and my focus were telling her that I thought the more money we had, the happier we'd be—and that her spending was ruining that. Yet it wasn't Bev who was hurting our relationship—it was me.

So I changed course, and for six months I didn't say anything about the credit card bills. Instead, I worked to communicate to her that I loved her and not money. I made an effort most days to write her love notes, and so on. After about eight months of this, I found my wife crying and

18 https://www.aarp.org/home-family/friends-family/info-2021/long-term-marriage-and-divorce.html

asked her what was wrong. She said that she'd realized she had been using the credit card to get back at me, because she felt I loved money more than her. She now realized that was not true.

Once she and I became united in our financial goals and financial management, we were able to strengthen our life together.

Money has an important role in life, and that is to be the wild card in the barter system. Unfortunately, we have greatly perverted its purpose. We now assume it is a major power source of life, but it's not powerful. Relationships are powerful, not money. The only reason money appears powerful is because most people believe it is. Remember, **"How you think about money will determine everything you will do *with* and *for* money."**

Tax Advice versus Tax Prep

I learned a lot during the years of 1981 to 1984 as I gained my CFP®/ CPA. As a CPA financial advisor, one thing I noticed was the difference between the concept of tax preparation and that of tax advice.

Tax preparation, a service offered by programs like TurboTax and H&R Block locations, is the process of correctly preparing tax forms. The goal of tax preparation is the accurate completion of the tax forms clients have due. There is no strategy associated with tax preparation. A tax preparer doesn't work to reduce your tax liability, increase a tax refund amount, or pave the way for lower future taxes. They simply enter the right information on the right line of forms provided by the IRS and then do the calculations as directed by the forms. This is a valid, helpful service, but it's important that it not be confused with tax advice.

For those individuals who have regular W-2 wages, no deductions to itemize, and a very straightforward return, tax preparation and programs like TurboTax can be great. But if there is any additional complexity to your income, saving, or spending, then you can miss out on substantial savings if you do not use a tax advisor.

Tax advice is a completely different discipline. Advice involves delving into a client's unique future goals, current finances, potential risks, and state-specific tax laws, and working to lower their tax liability strategically while also increasing savings both now and in the future. Whether this means maxing out health savings contributions, selecting a Roth IRA over a traditional IRA, managing and timing a Roth conversion, planning charitable contributions, or navigating state-specific tax pitfalls, a tax advisor has your back.

It's not unusual for me to meet with a client who happily does their own tax preparation year after year. Because they don't know what they should expect out of the end product, they are satisfied with knowing the data has been entered and the math was done right.

One of our clients, a man named Chuck, was content doing his own tax prep back in the 1990s when he came to us. Chuck is a frugal guy who thought that tax planning simply meant getting all the numbers right on his tax return. When we reviewed his last few years of returns, we found that he had paid a few thousand more in taxes every year than he might have if he'd had the right tax advisor involved. When we gave him tips on reducing his tax burden, he couldn't figure out how to get TurboTax to make the complex moves we suggested. We took over his tax planning, and he's never looked back.

Other client errors I've seen on self-prepared returns include treating 529 distributions for valid college expenses as taxable and avoiding itemizing federal returns because the standard deduction was slightly more—but not realizing this also meant they could NOT itemize state returns where the savings would have been substantial, especially true in MD.

Understanding the W-2 with emphasis on the codes in box 12 is one of the easy keys to lower taxes on a client's 1040. Knowing what the final tax return output should be is another key to tax advice.

Let's put it this way—a lot of returns I review yearly done by TurboTax have significant errors or missed tax-planning opportunities. Tax-preparer returns may have errors, and rarely ever mention tax-saving strategies. This should make you think about what kind of tax preparer you work with.

When looking for a financial professional who can treat your financial plan much like a medical doctor would treat your physical health, your goal should be to find one who can review your annual tax return. Remember, a tax preparer's job does not involve saving you any money on taxes. A tax advisor, however, is focused exclusively on that.

Volatility: A Necessary Evil

Finally, I want to talk about volatility, which is the abrupt, unpredictable price movement of securities. In the last chapter, I briefly mentioned that volatility is required if you're going to make a good rate of return. Volatility is directly related to risk, and the old saying, ***with great risk often comes great reward***, is true.

When investing in stocks, one of the ways to make a profit is by accepting volatility between the time you buy the position and the time you sell it. This unpredictable movement of volatility is the reason that stocks appear risky—but also the reason why they can help your portfolio accumulate so much value.

No investor or advisor can guarantee when a position will be up or down, and that can be scary. But that volatility is necessary to make a reasonable rate of return. You should be thankful for the volatility.

The risk associated with volatility is your psychological ability to watch the ebbs and flows. If you panic sell during the down times, it will lock in a loss and you are unlikely to buy back in the upswing. That's where an advisor who works like a doctor of personal finance comes in. With their help, you can come up with ways to gain peace of mind during periods of negative volatility.

A certificate of deposit comes with no volatility, but it currently yields very low returns. Higher volatility may give an incredible rate of return, but you need to understand *why* you're doing what you're doing. Diversify to tamper the volatility and allow it to work for you. Structure your portfolio in such a way that you can watch volatility over time without letting the fear component in.

It's also worth noting that volatility is different from momentum. Of momentum, somebody once said, "When something starts going in a direction, it'll keep going in that direction until it stops." That may sound like a ridiculously simple concept, but it's actually quite profound in the stock market. Because in the stock market, when something starts to go up, it'll keep going up unless something significant comes out and stops it.

Back in 2000, everybody thought that Amazon was ridiculously overvalued. It wasn't until 2010 and 2012 that people realized Amazon was ridiculously *undervalued,* and once people started to understand that, they drove it up to ridiculous amounts. So even if your intellect says, "I just can't see Amazon at seventy-five times earnings anymore," it doesn't matter. Because of the momentum, Amazon just keeps plowing ahead. Something has to happen to stop the momentum of a stock, in either direction.

This is one of the reasons index funds can be such a valuable investment. Index funds don't care about reasoning whether a stock should be rising and falling; they simply see what's got momentum and keep making it a larger percentage of the fund. Or, if the momentum reverses, they make the position a smaller part of the fund.

So the great stocks that continue to power ahead, like those that Warren Buffett likes to buy, continue to become bigger portions of the index. The stocks that have lost their power become a smaller portion of the index or are eliminated altogether. That's why index funds work so effectively, as compared to actively managed mutual funds.

The negative side of this is that there will come a day when everybody and his brother has decided that index funds are the only way to invest, and it won't work because by that time, anybody buying or selling individual positions will create immense volatility since the majority of people are just sitting in an index fund. So you always have to keep in mind whether index funds have gotten too popular.[19]

---

19 For more information about these topics and more, please visit the Financial Consulate's Knowledge Center: https://financialconsulate.com/knowledge-center/

Chapter 3

By late 1983, with my CPA and CFP° credentials in hand, I was ready to take the next step in my career and become a partner in Daniel's firm. After having worked with him for several years, I believed that he and I would make complementary partners and pursued a change to our deal. By that time, I was making more money than he was, but he was getting a piece of every sale I made, and we were struggling to hash out a fair partnership agreement.

Enter Terry Regan, a friend and golf partner. Terry later became my personal and company CPA, but in 1983 we were simply friends having dinner with our wives. I explained the issues I was having in hashing out the agreement with Daniel when Terry said, "Why are you trying to become partners with this guy if you're already producing more than him? What benefit is he bringing to you?"

With Terry's simple question lingering over the table, I was forced to realize that as much as I liked Daniel and respected him, Terry was right. This was a partnership in futility. So I decided to break free of Daniel and ask IM&R to give me my own branch office. IM&R agreed, and I formed my own company.

At this early point in my career, I wanted to move my practice from a solo salesperson to a company dedicated to professional financial advice. I decided to join forces with Kevin, a gifted technical mind I'd met in the Association of Financial Planning. We created a company under his already incorporated firm, Coordinated Asset Planning Company (CAPCO). I also took a colleague named Amy with me to do the marketing.

Kevin was a back office, number-crunching kind of guy. He wasn't the type to hit the streets and find clients. My hope was Amy would handle marketing, I would be the client-facing financial advisor, and Kevin would get all the behind-the-scenes work done writing financial plans and trading. It was my first attempt at forming a truly professional financial advisory firm.

What did I mean by that? My goal was to create a firm that ran how I thought a real financial advisory company should run. I didn't want it to be every man for himself, which was the prevailing principle of the industry at the time and is still prominent today.

There's a saying in the financial industry: eat what you kill. What that means is unless you can make a commission, unless you can make money selling clients, you're not going to eat. And that's foolishness. There are incredibly talented people out there who aren't much at sales who can help people tremendously with their personal finances, but they're not salespeople.

Thanks to the internet, these gifted, non-sales people have found a place to share their brilliance. One example is self-proclaimed financial planning "nerd" Michael Kitces. Not the least bit focused on selling products, Kitces labels himself a "financial *advicer*," and he focuses on using his experience and talents to help people understand how to make the best out of complex financial planning issues.

Of course, back in late 1984 to early 1985, this was unheard of. The industry was ruled by brokerages and insurers and banks, and it was completely focused on selling products. But I was already thinking differently. I had this dream that we could run a financial planning firm in a similar way to a legal firm or a medical practice. That, like lawyers and doctors, we wouldn't have to go out there constantly beating the streets just to find clients. Instead, we'd hire someone with talent to do the marketing, partner with tax planners, and offer extensive financial planning advice allowing all the employees in the firm to use their skills to benefit every client.

While I would eventually get there, let's just say CAPCO was not going to be the vehicle to transport me. It was, however, an important pit stop for helping me work out this vision and clarify my goals. Further, it introduced me to a vital medium—the radio.

On the Radio

One of the first things we needed to do to make CAPCO a success was to bring clients through the door. An ideal way to do this in 1984 was to get on the radio. That was the successful plan used by a local lawyer, Michael Hodes, who had a radio show to promote his elder care law practice. He was among the first in the Baltimore area to help people who had money get approved for Medicaid so they wouldn't drain all their assets for medical care during retirement.

On his show, Michael talked about general financial planning topics, and occasionally he'd invite other experts as guests. At that time, I was still the president of the Baltimore Association for Financial Planning, and one day, he invited me on the show.

The studio was straight out of the 1960s. Giant microphones, old technology, and a huge soundboard dominated the small space. While it was my first time on the radio, I had done numerous in-person presentations to groups like the top executives of McCormick and Company, or

Koppers Company with as many as 100 people in an auditorium. Being on the radio came naturally to me, and I really enjoyed it.

During the show, the topic of Maryland (MD) Savings and Loan Association (S&Ls) came up, and I talked about how these institutions may be doomed to go under. Michael, who had affiliations with MD S&Ls, challenged me on this. Pushed to explain my thought process, I happily did.[20]

In 1982 the MD S&Ls were only yielding about 1 percent more than federal S&Ls. By 1984, the spread had grown to 3 percent or more from federal equivalents. All investments compete against each other, so when one becomes more competitive by offering a higher yield than another, it's a warning flag that there's more risk involved in the higher-yield position. So you have to ask, why is that risk expanding? Why are they offering higher yields?

I knew from my study of financial history, nobody can survive a run on a market. Looking into it, I found that the MD S&Ls had an insurance program called the MSSIC backing them. MSSIC turned out to be a little entity that was not backed by anything other than an empty promise from the state of Maryland. This was concerning because Maryland can't print its own money. Therefore, the state's S&Ls had nothing to prevent a run on them, and since there was no real backing to them, a run would be existential.

When the FDIC backs something, you know that they've got the unconditional guarantee of the United States government, which actually prints the money. As long as the Federal Reserve agrees to print money to bail out banks when they go under, then the FDIC is as strong as the US government. MSSIC was an entity backed by a very empty promise from the state of Maryland, and the state of Maryland could only drain so much money out of its population, which meant when the thrifts had

---

20 Please see disclaimer on page 4.

a run on them, nobody was going to be able to stop it. Lo and behold, about five months later, the Maryland S&Ls went under.

What did the state of Maryland do? It stepped in and said they would back the S&L funds, but that the depositors were only allowed to take out $1,000 per month over the next four years.[21] The only exception to this was for those Maryland S&Ls that were approved to convert to federal S&Ls, which did not come close to including all institutions.

Fifteen years later, I had another thought based on the same principle.[22] Many big-named money market fund sponsors had loans default inside their money market funds. They bought the defaulted paper out at full price, took the loss to themselves, and put the money back into the account so they didn't have to say the money market fund broke the buck. Watching this, I guessed that sooner or later, somebody wouldn't be able to bail out that defaulted paper. If a fund could not bail out its money market fund and broke the buck, it may prompt a full-out panic.

The Reserve Fund did break the buck in 2008, and it caused a run on money market funds that only stopped when the Federal Reserve created a backstop to money funds.

Critical thinking as an advisor is like a doctor who looks at all the seemingly random symptoms you present at a visit and understands what illness you might be fighting. That is what any personal financial advisor should be able to do for their clients.

A Dream Takes Shape

With CAPCO, I was determined to create a more holistic model of financial planning. I'd bring in the client, and we'd collect all their paperwork and documents. We'd analyze assets and income and see if they

---

21 https://www.washingtonpost.com/archive/politics/1985/12/26/toothless-watch-dogs-share-the-blame/964dcca0-748e-4f73-9375-7acae72c9a8a/

22 Please see disclaimer on page 4.

were headed in the right direction for retirement. Often, we would find clients with poorly designed risk management and use of insurance. We would review their wills and tax returns to find the weaknesses and/or errors. We would then write a comprehensive personal financial strategy for their investing, saving, tax planning, estate planning, life insurance, property and casualty insurance, and so forth.

The difference in what I was doing for my clients compared to when I'd gotten my start with IDS was astounding. When I was with IDS, my goal was simply to find somebody who had money and put it into an annuity or similar product, earn a commission, and move on to the next client. As I got away from that model and pivoted into financial planning, I became more focused on understanding the client and their needs. Now, instead of having a very limited, company-specific product offering, I had access to a wide variety of investments and insurances.

Still, CAPCO wasn't yet doing as well as it could have been, and I was still struggling, in part because Amy, our marketing person, wasn't very good at setting up seminars and securing appointments with prospects. So around 1986, she left.

Kevin was the next person to leave the firm. A background number cruncher at heart, Kevin wanted to have a daily nine-to-five schedule, which wasn't practical as we tried to grow our business. In October 1987, the market crashed, and I was ready to dedicate long hours to growing the business, but Kevin wasn't. So, Kevin left the business, and I was left with the name Coordinated Asset Planning Company (CAPCO).

Black Monday

With Kevin gone, I worked to maintain client accounts while also keeping an eye on market trends and watching to see where history might repeat itself. In June 1987, before the crash, I had written a letter to clients that I was concerned that in 1988, the market might take a 500-point downturn in one day.[23]

As a lifelong student of the markets, I love studying them and reading about great investors. I also believe in patterns. By June 1987, I saw that the market had risen fast, possibly too quickly, almost as if there was a bit of mania driving the movement. When movement is this fast and seemingly manic, it's not unusual for a precipitous fall to begin quite quickly. The funny thing was that many large financial groups had created program trading that said:

- if X happens, buy; or
- if Y happens, sell.

In October 1987, the programs got a Y, and they all tried to sell. My thinking seemed smart on October 19, 1987, when all the gains made during the prior nine months were lost on Black Monday, but the problem was I thought this wouldn't happen until 1988. It taught me a great lesson about trying to predict what markets may do. You may get one thing right about the market, but not everything, which makes predictions about short-term markets worthless.

Tools for Financial Planning

In this chapter, I've illustrated how my early career began to take shape as I worked to model myself like a doctor of personal finance and build a firm opposite of the idea that financial advisors must be more focused on sales than on planning.

Part of my goal at CAPCO was to be a great employer, so I want to close the chapter talking about how to maximize the benefits a great employer offers. I also want to talk about how you can explore your biases,

---

23 Please see disclaimer on page 4.

something too few people do as investors, especially with today's political propaganda from both sides of the aisle polluting rational investing considerations.

Finally, I want to talk about how listening to the investing universe can help you avoid poor investments.

- Exploring your own biases
- Maximizing employee benefits
- Listening to the investing universe

Exploring Your Own Biases

Earlier in the book, I talked about how you wouldn't want biased medical advice from your doctor, so why would you want biased investing advice from your financial advisor? But it's not just advisor bias you need to worry about. You also need to think about your own bias.

As I've said before, the way you think about money will determine everything you are going to do *with* and *for* money. How do you discover your own biases? One of the things you can do that is very helpful is sit down and write out what your experiences with money have been. Then, push further. What have your experiences been with taxes and the IRS? How did your parents handle money? Were they spenders or savers? Did you have any traumas in your life with money? Did you ever get fired from a job and worry about how you were going to make ends meet? Did you ever have trouble paying for a service you needed? How have all these events and experiences affected how you feel about money today?

Recently, we had a client come to our firm who had about $60,000 sitting in a savings account. I suggested we move $14,000 (the limit for her and her husband) to Roth IRAs. She immediately objected to this plan. When I asked her why, she said that the money she'd saved was her "dog fund," for potential veterinary or other pet-related expenses. She also noted that she would need a new car sometime in the next two years. Finally, she mentioned that she'd once lost her job and was traumatized by the experience. Since then, she has always made sure she had enough money available to make ends meet should that happen again.

It was extremely helpful to have insight into her resistance to making a Roth contribution. It also allowed me to ease her fears, letting her know that if we put the $14,000 into Roths, she could always take that back out and have it in two to three days without any taxes or penalties. (Contributions come out of Roth IRA accounts first penalty-free and tax-free, no matter your age). Once she understood this, she was happily able to take advantage of the potential tax savings and tax-free growth offered by the Roth.

Don't be afraid to confront yourself over your own biases. Talk to an experienced, credentialed advisor about your concerns and how they may be related to your personal fears and experiences. You may be surprised to learn how their planning can help you find solutions to handle your money the right way without the anxieties and triggers you've grown used to.

Just make sure that advisor is independent, fee-only, and a fiduciary, or their biases may counteract yours.

Maximizing Employee Benefits

Like most things in life, employee benefits have their good and bad points. Your goal is to maximize those benefits that are worthwhile and avoid those that aren't. Yes, quite a few employer benefits may be worthless to you.

Group Term Life Insurance

You can't assume that just because your employer's offering a benefit that it's advantageous to take it. The greatest example of this is group supplemental life insurance (the amount you buy over the free coverage paid for by your employer). Group supplemental life insurance is of no benefit to anyone, unless you're a smoker or have frequent or chronic illnesses.

If an insurance company is going to approve every worker who signs up for group life insurance without question or testing, then higher-risk people, such as those who smoke, are severely overweight, or those previously diagnosed with potentially life-threatening conditions, are combined with lower-risk people. Yet the term premiums are priced the same for everyone in the company based on age bands of five-year increments. In essence, healthy employees are subsidizing the riskier employees by being a part of the employer plan.

In the private market, the healthiest people get rock-bottom rates while riskier people pay either significantly higher rates or are denied coverage altogether. With private insurance, you could easily pay as much as 50 percent less premium than what you're paying with group supplemental life insurance.

In addition, with your own policy, you get to keep the coverage if you decide to move to another company. With group insurance, you lose the coverage when you leave the employer. And since you're likely older at that point than you were when you first got group coverage, a new individual policy will have a higher premium than it would have if you had secured it at a younger age.

Lastly, group supplemental life insurance generally has a significant increase in premium every five years. With a private policy, your premium is locked in for the entire term of the coverage.

Your employer's *free* group life insurance has no downside. It is free, but since you may lose that coverage when you leave your company, remember to supplement the free policy with private insurance you own to lock in rates at a younger age.

Group Disability

An employer benefit that's less clear cut is group disability. The problem with group disability is the way the policy defines disability. For the first two years of coverage, a group disability policy will generally define disabled as being unable to perform the tasks related to their own occupation.[24] This is a clear-cut, limited definition that is generally in an insured's best interests.

After two years, however, a group disability policy will redefine disabled as being unable to perform any occupation, which by training, education, or experience, the insured is able to do.[25] This broader definition of disabled makes it much harder to continue getting benefits since it broadens the type of work the insured must be unable to do.

This change in disability definition is definitely a downside but may be worth taking simply because group disability is so much more affordable. Individual disability policies—which will generally keep that first definition of disabled—are much more expensive, often prohibitively so.

While individual policies are definitely a better choice for most, their premiums often make them an impractical option. In many cases, we advise clients to consider their employer-sponsored disability policy for their risk management but also to save rainy-day money to compensate for losses in benefits as the definition of disability changes.

Another possible advantage of employer-sponsored group disability policies is that the benefit may be tax-free, depending on how the premium is paid. If the company pays the premium but passes on the tax liability

24 https://www.nolo.com/legal-encyclopedia/understanding-your-long-term-disability-policy.html
25 https://www.ama-assn.org/residents-students/career-planning-resource/evaluating-disability-policy

of payments onto employees, it allows future benefits to be tax-free. If the insured doesn't pay the taxes on the premium, the benefits are 100 percent taxable.[26]

To understand how big an impact this can make, let's consider a group disability policy paying a benefit equal to 60 percent of your gross $100,000 income. If you get that benefit for ten years and you've already paid the taxes on the premiums going into the policy, you would receive $60,000 tax-free income yearly for ten years.

If you are not paying the taxes on the premiums, then you still get the $60,000 payout yearly, but you have to pay taxes on that amount—rather than the much lower premium payments. The true effect of this would depend on how much total income your family's bringing in. Someone making $100,000 who goes on disability and gets a taxable $60,000 benefit is going to lose at least $6,000 every year, more if they live in an area with state income taxes.

Some people might argue that a taxable disability benefit opens up the opportunity to do Roth IRAs, but that will generally be a trivial benefit when you consider the taxes paid on the disability income. And what if you have other income, such as Social Security? This could bump your income high enough that your Social Security benefits become taxable.

At the end of the day, a tax-free disability income is likely going to net you the most advantages. The key is to have the employer tax your premium payment each year as part of your taxable wages. This normally ranges from $500 to $800 per year for someone making around $100,000.

---

26 https://www.irs.gov/faqs/interest-dividends-other-types-of-income/life-insurance-disability-insurance-proceeds/life-insurance-disability-insurance-proceeds-1

Critical Illness and Hospital Benefits

Many employers tout critical illness, cancer, and hospitalization policies as a benefit. They may position these benefits as risk management, but really, they are simply a morbid form of gambling. Risk management is not trying to insure against specific health risks we all face—that would be ridiculous.

What you need is comprehensive medical insurance and a sound disability strategy that includes insurance to protect from **any** illness or accident. To isolate insurance for cancer, accidents, or a hospital stay is not sound risk management. People may benefit from these types of coverage, but they are a waste of money in a sound risk management strategy.

Health Savings Account (HSA)

When you want to consider the great benefits offered by an employer, a health savings account (HSA) is definitely one of them. In fact, I'd say it's the best benefit of all. Do not confuse the health savings account with a use-it-or-lose-it flexible spending medical account (FSA). The FSA is a trivial benefit for someone who knows significant medical bills, like children's braces, are going to be paid in a particular year. Compared to the HSA, you will understand why the FSA is trivial.

The HSA is a tax-favored health savings account that can only be used in conjunction with an HSA-qualified, high-deductible health plan (HDHP). Employers and employees can both contribute to an HSA.[27] Even if your employer doesn't contribute, this plan can be a critical part of your medical future. If you're single, as of 2022, you can contribute $3,650. If you have a family plan, you can contribute $7,300.[28] Those

---

27 https://www.irs.gov/publications/p969

28 https://www.healthcare.gov/glossary/health-savings-account-hsa/

who are over fifty-five can also contribute an additional $1,000 catch-up contribution.

Not only do you get a tax deduction for the contribution and tax-deferred growth once it's in the account, but if it's withdrawn to pay qualifying medical expenses, the distribution is tax-free.

Another point in the HSA's favor is that it's cumulative. In other words, you can keep accruing that money, tax-free, for decades. When you leave your employer or retire, you still get to keep the funds, as they are not subject to a vesting schedule.[29]

The funds in your HSA can also be used to pay your Medicare Part B and Part D premiums, long-term care premiums, vision and dental expenses, drugs, medical equipment, and disability-accommodating home improvements.[30]

The only thing you can't use an HSA for is a health insurance premium, Medicare supplement, or Medigap plan premiums.

I have relatively healthy clients who have been contributing to their HSAs for seven or eight years. With the tax-free accumulation and appropriate investment options, they've grown as much as $100,000 savings for future medical use. You can't imagine how many nuances there are to the HSA that makes them so dynamic to have.

The HSA can be just as valuable to a person who has chronic illnesses and is paying a lot of money every year in medical bills. It can allow you to choose a high-deductible plan that saves you thousands in premiums each year while also giving you a tax advantage on the dollars you pull from the HSA to pay that deductible.

Should an individual pass away before using all the funds in their HSA, their beneficiary still has one year to keep the HSA open and use funds to repay existing medical bills the individual leaves behind.

---

29 https://www.forbes.com/sites/ericbrotman/2019/11/26/open-enrollment-is-coming-consider-an-hsa/?sh=3591f9c77a3f

30 p502.pdf

Anything left over in the account after that is general taxable income to the beneficiary, just as it would be if it were in an IRA.

401(k) Match

Believe it or not, many people don't bother with a company-offered 401(k) match. While there are times when it makes sense not to, a 401(k) with a match is generally a great way to get free money. If you have a 401(k) with a plan match, I suggest participating at least to the percent of salary that gives you the full matching contribution.

Employer Stock Purchase Plan (ESPP)

When you work for a large, publicly traded company with an ESPP, you can buy company stock at a discount from the market price. The discount may be on the market price at purchase, or it may be based on an average price over a set period. If you like your company, then buying your company stock in an ESPP would be a wise consideration.

Stock Options

Stock options allow you to buy company stock at a set price, regardless of what it's trading for in the market. For example, ABC stock may be trading for $15 a share in the market, but if you work for them, you may have been given an option to buy ABC at $10 a share anytime during a ten-year period. The difference between what you buy it for and what it's selling for in the market is considered your option *gain*.

There are two types of stock options: qualified and nonqualified. With a qualified stock option, you don't have to report the option gains on an exercised option as wage income, as long as you keep the stock for at least a year.[31] After the year, once you sell, you pay long-term capital

---

31 This may trigger the alternative minimum tax, so consult with a tax planner before making any decisions.

gains tax. If you don't hold it for a year and instead sell it before the year is out, you'll need to pay ordinary income tax on the option gain.

The gains on nonqualified stock options, on the other hand, are taxable as wage income, no matter what. This means once exercised, even if you hold the position, you must pay state and local taxes, as well as Social Security and Medicare on the difference between the market price per share and the option price per share.

Although this can be a difficult pill to swallow, there are ways to potentially minimize the amount of tax paid. For instance, if you think the company's stock will eventually rise exponentially, it may be worth it to exercise your options when you have enough gain to buy and hold the stock, thus minimizing your earned income upon exercise. You then hold the stock and sell later at potentially much higher prices and only pay capital gains on the difference.

My general rule is to exercise stock options within one to two years of expiration, because even the most optimistic company can swoon in price in a bear market for a year or two.

Restricted Stock Units

Some companies offer restricted stock units as a form of compensation to employees. Since they are restricted, an employee doesn't receive the stocks until they meet certain service year requirements. The value of the stock, when vested, is considered wage income to the employee, so they can expect to pay Social Security, Medicare tax, federal, state, and local income taxes on each vested value.

Because there is no way to avoid taxes on restricted stocks, it's critical that you have an effective tax strategy when they're offered to you. That's where an 83(b) election comes in. This election, made on an IRS form, allows you to choose whether to be taxed on the stock units/shares once they are granted, before being vested. If you think that the company is going to rise substantially in value, then it could be well worth paying tax on the stocks at today's value and tax rate, rather than waiting a few years until you receive the stocks.

Remember, an 83(b) election requires you to pay the tax implications today before you have even vested, so you may never get the stock if you leave before the vesting time frame. That is why you need to:

1. Believe the stock will rise **substantially;** and

2. Intend to be with the company through the full vesting time.

The 83(b) election is a complicated decision, and it's best to make it with an experienced tax planner and comprehensive advisor.

Deferred Compensation

Some employers offer to defer a portion of their employees' compensation to a later date. This pushes forward their income tax and other liabilities and can be an effective method of retirement saving.

Employees considering this option must be extremely careful to measure whether it's worth the risk. What risk? Well, when you defer compensation, you become a general creditor of the company. These funds are not protected like a 401(k) or pension plan, so if the company files bankruptcy, the deferred compensation could disappear.

In addition, employees need to consider carefully which distribution schedule to receive their deferred compensation. Employees may be able to schedule receipt during their career or after retirement, but once they've made the election, it's very difficult to change.

There are many reasons the distribution schedule matters, but one example is for those employees who plan to move to lower-tax states upon retirement. If they choose a five-year election and begin to receive the payout the year they retire, the compensation will likely be issued as taxable income in the state they worked in, even if they move during that five-year period. If they choose a ten-year or longer payout, then the income taxation of the distribution follows them to the state where they relocate.

Whatever benefits your employer offers, it's well worth your time to read and understand them and consult with a knowledgeable, fee-only, professional advisor to create a strategy around their structure. That way you can take advantage of every worthwhile benefit, skipping those that don't make sense for your situation and maximizing those that do.

Listening to the Investing Universe

Earlier in this chapter, I pointed out that the spread between the Maryland S&L interest rate and the federal S&L interest rate was at the root of my prediction of failure. It may sound especially prescient, but it's actually an easy prediction to make when you consider one important truth—all investments compete against the safest investment out there, which, for a US citizen, is a US Treasury bill.

Think about it this way: If the United States Treasury bill was yielding 10 percent, and you felt that the stock market had 10 percent upside potential, would you ever invest in the stock market? Of course not—why would you accept the volatility and risk of the stock market when you could get the same return guaranteed?

In short, you wouldn't make an investment that's yielding the same as the United States Treasury bill *unless there was something about it that made it worthwhile*, like tax-free municipal bonds.

When you see an investment's promised returns leaping ahead of the return of the safest investment available, it's an indication that **risk** is present. When the Maryland S&Ls, which were only backed by the empty shell of the MSSIC, raised their interest rates so significantly over those of the federal S&Ls, which were backed by the Federal Savings and Loan Insurance Corporation, it was a clear indication of a problem.

So remember this: in the universe of investing, spread between rates is an indication of risk. Make sure you know how to evaluate risk, or have someone you trust assist you.[32]

---

32 For more information about these topics and more, please visit the Financial Consulate's Knowledge Center: https://financialconsulate.com/knowledge-center/

Chapter 4

After navigating the crash of 1987 and with Kevin and Amy both gone from CAPCO, I began my next attempt to build a professional advisory firm.

A Raymond James advisor named Roland and I formed a joint venture. Rather than leaping into another partnership, we simply shared an office and decided to test the waters around a joint endeavor.

Around this time, an old friend named Chris O'Shea, who was sick of the corporate world, decided he wanted to see if he could make a bigger difference by working with a small firm. I had known Chris, a CPA, since the early 1970s. His brother Bill, who I'd worked with after leaving IDS, had been my best friend since the ninth grade, and Chris was working on his CPA credential, so it seemed like a no-brainer to bring him on.

In the beginning, Chris focused on doing tax returns with my firm as side work, but by 1989, he joined me full time. This turned out to be one of the best decisions I ever made because while he and I were like oil and water, we always brought out the best in each other and attacked each problem from a different perspective, ensuring that well-rounded solutions were eventually reached.

One such solution was the development of the **Financial Physical™**. The financial planning process (for most) back in the 1980s generally started by collecting all the data you could from clients, including their total debt, assets, insurance policies, and so on. Advisors would then take this information and enter it into a computer program, which would spit out a ream of paper containing planning recommendations based on the barest minimum information.

Advisors would then bind these papers and meet with the client, picking out the key elements necessary to add to the financial plan, such as a life insurance or long-term care policy. Naturally, the advisor would be able to sell all those recommended products, ultimately earning a commission.

These plans consisted only of generic advice suitable for any person who came through the door. Can you imagine if you went to your doctor, and they printed out a stack of papers for you and told you the same thing they'd told the last five patients who came into the office? Just like if your doctor were to do this, the generic financial information provided by these computers was practically worthless. Computer-generated financial plans are still very common today.

Chris and I thought that a true financial advisor should have the knowledge to develop customized plans for their clients, plans that considered what the client actually needed for their goals, their lifestyle, and their situation. Further, we felt that advisors should have a widespread knowledge of all the different financial instruments—including those they could earn no commission on—to offer client-specific recommendations that really made a difference.

Instead, advisors were just sending stuff off to these computer centers, and the computer center would send back all this paperwork, and they'd take the paperwork and sell the client a bunch of mutual funds and insurance policies.

By 1990, Chris and I knew that this standardized, computer-generated planning was insufficient for our clients. It wasn't totally worthless, but it wasn't enough. I wanted to go deeper. I wanted the planning experience to be similar to a checkup with a good doctor.

One day, I said to Chris, "Why don't we do financial planning like a doctor would do medicine? We can collect their information for diagnostics, but also get more from them—a handle on their goals, their dreams, and financial aspirations for themselves and their family. Then, we'll tell them what we're seeing and what we think they need to do—not just about commission-paying products we think we can sell them. When they come back, we'll give them a written description of our thoughts and recommendations."

It was at that point that the Financial Physical™ was born. Just as a doctor knows all parts of the human anatomy, I think a financial advisor should know everything there is to know about money, insurance, company benefits, estate planning, income taxes, elder care, retirement planning, college planning, and so on.

Likewise, as a doctor takes a full physical history for their new patients, I think an advisor should take a full financial history for their new clients—and that's what the Financial Physical™ allowed us to do.

Enter Schwab

During these years, an interval lasting from about 1984 to 1995, I was a licensed representative of Raymond James. I was consistently in the top fifty brokers, rewarded with company-paid trips. This meant jaunting to far-flung locales such as Switzerland, Kenya, Sweden, and Eastern Europe, all expenses paid by Raymond James and other commission product providers.

But by 1993, the shine had worn off, and I made a frustrating realization. It was during a trip to Eastern Europe, staying in a well-appointed hotel room on the company's dime when I turned to my wife and said, "Do you know who's paying for this trip? The clients." I found it unacceptable that clients would be charged so much in commissions that the brokerage could afford to pay for trips for their advisors. After all, we already got paid commissions on the planning moves we made for clients, a practice I already had qualms about.

Right around this time, Schwab had come out with a trading platform that allowed independent investment advisors to put some of their client business through them on a fee-only basis.[33] Schwab had always been a company I held in high esteem. The company arose out of Charles Schwab's personal desire to benefit clients at a time when he felt that the research being released by brokerage firms was faulty. So, he started his own research firm in 1963 and launched his investment advisory newsletter.[34]

In 1971, he started the brokerage arm to begin buying and selling stocks and other investments for clients. At the time Schwab began its investment services, brokerage firms were regulated, and the amount of commissions they could charge was firmly capped. By 1974, the SEC experimented with deregulating certain securities transactions, and by 1975 the caps on commissions were off.

While other brokerages at this time quickly raised their commission rates and added new fees, Schwab didn't. In fact, Schwab *decreased* their commissions from their former rates by 70 percent and created the first discount brokerage.[35]

I kept most business with Raymond James but began testing out the Schwab platform and the fee-only approach. This would prove to be a career-changing move.

Taking Over Radio

Since my first stint on the radio in 1984, I had maintained a steady presence as a guest on various shows. In 1991, I went to WCBM Baltimore

---

33 https://www.aboutschwab.com/history
34 https://www.aboutschwab.com/history
35 https://www.latimes.com/archives/la-xpm-1985-04-28-fi-21560-story.html

and asked to advertise on radio host Tom Marr's weekday show. We worked out an advertising deal that included having me stop by as a guest on the show every once in a while.

The first time he invited me on the show was in 1991. The big topic at that time was Operation Desert Storm, after Iraq invaded Kuwait.[36] Marr thought war was going to be a big negative for markets, and I disagreed. Markets, from a financial standpoint, do not always fear war. I thought it possible that the day the offensive into Iraq began might be the day the stock market took off.[37] Marr said that was ridiculous, that markets wouldn't go up if there was a war.

My gut told me they might, simply because this operation would help the world see that Saddam Hussein was bluffing, and once everyone realized this, the markets might move higher.

I was only on the show for about fifteen or twenty minutes, but during the first three hours after my appearance, our office received eighty phone calls from new potential clients. Over the next few days, we received fifty more.

At that point, Chris and I knew that we needed to stay on the radio, and since no one was doing professional financial shows at that time, we decided to work toward having our own show. There were financial shows of people selling products, just as there are today, but none dedicated to comprehensive advice.

Two years later in 1993, we were given a Thursday slot at 6:00 p.m.—prime drive time. We called our show *A Wealth of Advice* and used Pink Floyd's "Money" as our theme song. We paid for the one-hour show, but it was worth it. From that point forward, we got 80 percent of our business from that show.

The show was eventually moved to Wednesday nights when retired governor Schaefer asked WCBM for the Thursday night slot—a change

---

36 https://www.history.com/this-day-in-history/bush-orders-operation-desert-shield
37 Please see disclaimer on page 4.

we were not asked if we would accept but were simply told would happen. A fantastic reminder for us to stay humble.

We also were able to bring on many notable guests, including investor and prolific financial author Jim Rogers, international value investor and senior investment advisor to First Eagle Funds Jean-Marie Eveillard, Charles Schwab, and creator of the Templeton Growth Fund, Sir John Templeton. Sir John had no need to come on my radio show, but graciously gave us his time. He was the epitome of humility and kindness.

Spiritual Growth

By 1995, our radio show was in full swing and business was steady. In addition to being a time of growth in business and radio, this was a time of tremendous spiritual maturation for Chris and me.

While Chris explored the possibility of becoming a pastor, I was about to rededicate my Sundays to God. This happened thanks to my stepdaughter, Melania, who, in 1989, was working as an EMT. One day, she was called to a double motorcycle accident in which no one was wearing helmets. While she worked on one of the drivers, he called her his angel. What struck Melania was just how calm and present the injured man was after such a major accident.

A few days later, she couldn't stop thinking about his ability to stay calm, so she went to see him in the hospital, and after his release, they began to date. One day she asked him how he was able to be so controlled and present. He said it was because of a friend of his. When my stepdaughter said she wanted to meet this friend, he explained that the friend was Jesus.

She said, "You mean, that fictional man from the story?"

The young man looked at her and said, "Jesus is not fiction." The confidence and faith with which he said that helped bring Melania to an eventual spiritual awareness about God.

As Bev watched her daughter transform over the next few years, she started to attend church with her. One snowy Sunday morning in 1995, with the weather getting in the way of my usual golf plans, Bev suggested I go to church with them. I did and immediately felt the presence of God sitting right next to me. I heard God that day say, "You are no longer golfing on Sundays but instead coming to this church to learn from these people."

I did exactly that, and three years later, I quit our country club because I believed golf had become my idol.

We were proud of Melania and honored to see her blossom. At the same time, we had the delight of watching my stepson, Austin, embrace his inner entrepreneur. Austin joined the Marine Corps at eighteen years old, just after high school graduation.

Bev and I proudly watched as he persevered through everything thrown at him in training on Parris Island. During this time, I wrote to Austin often, reminding him that staying motivated and focused through these early difficult times would be instrumental in helping him get through other challenges in life.

After his time in the military, Austin managed a chain of video stores operating throughout Maryland and Florida and then decided to branch out on his own. He took the lessons he'd learned about business and transitioned that success into an impressive career as a wise dealmaker.

Watching my stepchildren flourish not only made me proud, but it was a continued reminder of how important family is—not just to me, but to my clients.

Becoming Fee-Only

By the middle of 1993, after four years with Roland, Chris and I realized we were not headed in the same direction. We wanted to be fee-only while Roland wanted to stay with Raymond James and remain fee- and commission-focused. There's nothing necessarily wrong with this choice;

it simply wasn't what Chris and I were focused on doing. So, we moved out and began the planning to become a fee-only Registered Investment Advisor (RIA) and drop all licenses to sell investments and insurance.

This was the start of a very big transition for us. Roland was gracious about our leaving, even though the bills we had been sharing would now be his alone. At the same time, Bev—who'd been working with us for ten years—decided to retire. Now, we had to find a replacement. On top of that, I lost half of my revenue to make the move to fee-only.

One of the fascinating things I noticed once I left Raymond James and moved all my business to Schwab was that, instead of spending client money sending top advisors on all-expenses-paid trips, Schwab threw one conference each year and made their advisors pay to attend. This highlighted to me the difference between Schwab and other brokers. Schwab was truly interested in providing the best, most affordable service to clients. **My business was finally where it belonged.**

A primary reason Roland wasn't on board with the idea of leaving Raymond James was because he had a tremendous amount of residual commissions coming in each year. An industry standard, these ongoing commissions are paid annually on certain renewable products, such as insurance policies. I think that the chief reason most advisors won't go fee-only is that they will lose residual commissions. Some advisors receive thousands of dollars in residual income each year—an income that requires very little ongoing work from them.

While you might have to give up residuals once you become fee-only, advisors still make an extremely good living doing so. Better yet, we make that living doing what's right for the client. If more advisors did this, we would see this industry change for the better. There is nothing worse than having a new client come in and seeing that other advisors pushed and recommended products without regard for what was in their best interests, and that it was perfectly legal to do so.

The financial industry should demand more from its advisors and brokerages. Our work should not be about chasing Rockefeller's famed "one more dollar." It should be about helping clients manage their money, goals, and legacy in a way that's best suited to them. Like doctors of personal finance. In doing so, we also earn a very generous living.

For my firm, it's all about reframing the practice of financial advising and moving away from being financial product managers to being true holistic wealth advisors. This involves finding out what each client's idea of wealth is—because it's not just about money. It could be about a legacy. It could be about an early retirement. It could be about travel. It could be about a lot of things that are *funded* by dollars, but not exclusively about accrual or accumulation.

Tools for Financial Planning

This chapter explored the continued refinement of my advisory firm from commission-focused to fee-only. It introduced the concept of residuals as a reason some advisors might not want to go fee-only and talked about my on-air prediction about the Iraq war being good for the stock market.

Now, let's see how some of these topics translate into tools you can use for your financial planning.

- Keeping away from the Joneses
- Avoid overspending
- The market voting machine

Keeping Away from the Joneses

It's possible that reluctance of some advisors to give up residuals is about their own spending issues. One of the roots of this problem could be caused by the feeling that they need to keep up certain appearances. I remember one Raymond James colleague proclaiming that buying the biggest house, the best car, and the most expensive toys would motivate an advisor to find the biggest clients. Well sure, but is that a good idea?

We've all heard about the phenomenon of keeping up with the Joneses—a humorous way to say that someone spends money to prove that they have as much as another person or family. You may think that you are above doing this, but this mindset is more pernicious than we think.

It's important to spend some time considering *why* you do the things you do. It's likely you will find at least one decision you've made that has been motivated by a need to "keep up" with someone else—perhaps a neighbor, friend, family member, or coworker. When you realize this, you need to ask yourself why status in this area is so important to you.

With the rise of social media, the need to spend as much (or more) as others in your circle has gotten even more insidious. With Facebook, Instagram, TikTok, and other sites, we constantly see every single financial decision people make. Even without social media, the drive to keep up appearances is constant, especially when you have children. One of the hardest positions to take is as the parent who says their child can't have a toy or device that all the other children have.

We also see this a lot in parents of college-age kids. Many parents are devoted to the idea of giving their kids a college experience they won't soon forget, because maybe the parents themselves always wanted that but didn't get it, or maybe because they had it and think it's something their children need too. The problem is that while the grandparents had the money to make that happen, the parents of the younger generation might not. By refusing to acknowledge that there are limits to what you can provide for your children, the real victim is you and your retirement.

Instead of borrowing money to help your kids, or stopping retirement contributions while they're in college, or even borrowing from your equity or retirement savings, remember that numbers don't lie—and your cash flow analysis that we talked about in Chapter 1 contains all the numbers you need to tell you what you can actually afford to do for your college-age children.

Avoid Overspending

Helping your kids with their college expenses can either be the most affordable thing you'll ever do, or it could bankrupt you. If you tell your children what you can afford, it's extremely affordable. If you let your children choose any college they want to go to, it can absolutely bankrupt you. The best rule of thumb is to let your budget lead the conversation.

Yet, so often we see parents taking their children on tours of colleges way outside their level of affordability, deciding that they'll "find a way" to make it happen. Too many times I've seen parents borrowing money, draining their home equity credit lines, their cash flow, or their retirement accounts in order to "make it happen." Some go years not saving, paying down debt, or contributing to retirement plans.

The worst part is, except for a few unique college degrees like engineering, an undergraduate degree from a prestigious school means very little. When your children graduate from college with a bachelor's degree, most employers don't care where they went to school. A prestigious school does not open the door for your kids to get a CPA or CFP˚ credential, get a law degree, go to medical school, or get an MBA any more than any other accredited university will. It's what the student does *after* graduating from college that makes a difference.

Look at the statistics—even graduating from a school like Harvard doesn't make an overall difference in earnings.[38] So why are we so focused on it?

---

38 https://www.huffpost.com/entry/the-surprising-fact-of-an-ivy-league-degree_b_59e12472e4b02e99c5835654

For some parents, it's not about buying college prestige so much as giving their kids the *college experience* and connections that can help them secure a good job after graduation. There used to be a time when graduating from the right college could have made a big difference in life, but around the mid-1980s, that totally flipped, and now graduating from *any* college is a good thing, so don't waste a bunch of money on it.[39]

In recent years, college costs have risen exorbitantly. Students, and parents, are getting stuck with six-figure debts for degrees that can only help a graduate earn $60,000 to $80,000 per year.[40] It very rarely, if ever, makes sense to pay a tuition that so far outweighs the earnings potential of the degree.

The buck stops with you, the parents. Because the bank and the university are not going to stop your children from borrowing too much for a degree in a field that pays too little. And when your children decide to get that expensive degree and you cosign on the loan, you're the only loser in the story.

You're the one who gets socked with the debt, on top of what you're trying to accumulate for retirement. You can't get the debt discharged in bankruptcy, and only you—not your children—have the assets to cover the debt, leaving you stuck. You can cross your fingers for debt forgiveness to come from the government, but private loans may not be eligible for forgiveness.[41]

As mentioned in the last section, the key is to determine what you can afford to contribute to your child's college education expenses, and let that be the limit you set for yourself. If that means they can go to state university and live at home and they want to do something different, then they can make up the difference by working or taking out a loan.

39 https://www.nber.org/papers/w7322

40 top-jobs-career-regret-student-debt

41 https://www.businessinsider.com/personal-finance/will-private-student-loans-be-forgiven

The case may differ if your children are athletes, since this may open up a wealth of new scholarship opportunities.

Ultimately, the way to make sure college costs don't spell financial disaster for you is to know what you can afford and control your contribution based on that. Some potential strategies include having your children attend a community college for the first two years and spend the last two at a university, or join the military to take advantage of the GI Bill, a straight path to long-term success since many employers prioritize these military college candidates.

College isn't the only overspending misstep we see clients make. As is very often the case, one of the biggest financial mistakes people make is also one of the simplest. It's not about investing in risky derivatives or following a spurious stock tip; it's about overspending on cars and houses.

Don't get me wrong—a wisely chosen house is a fantastic investment. The right property can easily hold its value or even appreciate, creating a comfortable profit. But to get there, you can't just buy any house in any area for any amount and do anything you want with it. You have to look for a good deal in a good area, maintain the house, and limit customized renovations so the property doesn't exclusively cater to your unique situation and needs.

Cars are very often an unadulterated waste of money. Once again, the ultimate financial goal is to find a way to live for today while still remembering that tomorrow is going to show up. I'm not suggesting that anyone drive an uncomfortable, unsafe car. But does your comfort level really require that $90,000 BMW, or can you be happy and comfortable in a $45,000 Toyota Highlander? Do you have to trade the car in every few years, or can you safely drive it until it reaches 150,000, 200,000, or more miles? These days, a well-made car with proper ongoing maintenance can easily last 150,000 miles or more, so remember to be prudent and evaluate your motivations for car purchases and trade-ins.

A lot of this depends on your net worth. Someone worth $30 million may be comfortable buying a $250,000 Porsche. But when you are worth a few million dollars, a greater percentage of wealth is eaten up by an expensive vehicle.

It isn't just the cost of a vehicle that's dangerous. Selling a vehicle every two or three years to get the latest and greatest is also a large expense. Some people assume that leasing is a good, cost-effective way to own the latest in auto technology, but leases are very complicated financial instruments that can easily manipulate the inexperienced lessee.

The Market Voting Machine

The last thing I want to talk about in this chapter is the importance of having a long-term investing strategy rather than a short-term habit of reaction. Economist and value-investing leader Benjamin Graham once said that on a regular basis, markets are a voting machine, yet are a weighing machine over the long term.[42] By that, he meant that the greed and fear investors have surrounding a company is measured by its daily stock trades, but the real intrinsic value of a company is assessed over the long-term performance.

Every day, people buy and sell stocks. These moves are a classic example of a voting machine; they show you what's popular, what's got the most appeal, and whose website has the most interest. Those are popularity contests, and that's what happens with stocks on a day-to-day basis.

While you'll hear the media give reasons for the market being up or down on a particular day, the truth is that there was a popularity contest and people bought or sold. If they sold more than they bought, the market's down. If they bought more than they sold, then it's up.

Now, if you look at the pattern of stocks over long periods, they show you what the weighing machine is really saying under the surface—and

---

42 https://news.morningstar.com/classroom2/course.asp?docId=142901&page=7

that is what counts. Are smart investors accumulating stocks, or are they liquidating stocks? If they're liquidating stocks, then the trend is going to be a bear market. If they're accumulating stocks, then the trend is going to be a bull market. That's the weighing machine.

The real evaluation of what a company is worth is based on the growth of its revenue, the control of its expenses, its profit, and the company's accumulation of wealth. So when the weighing machine looks at a company, it's about measuring the long-term growth of profits. How do you determine what value a company's long-term earnings will be? This is where things get complicated.

Warren Buffett used to do it Ben Graham's way, based on book value, but that had limitations. He needed a more sophisticated way to look beyond what everyone else saw. Enter Charlie Munger, who taught Buffett to look for companies that have great moats around them. In investing, a "moat" means some kind of advantage that can keep the company outperforming its competitors. Looking for a moat means looking for those companies with a firm grasp on their business where revenues can continue to grow, facing very few threats to their position in the markets. (Past examples include Apple and Microsoft, but keep your eyes open for moats that can eventually be crossed.)

As an investor, your goal is not to try to profit from the day-to-day popularity contest of the market. If you get caught up on the short-term dips and jumps, you miss out on the long-term evaluations. When a stock dips in value today, all that means is that more people sold than bought it on that day. Buying great companies for the long-term is how real wealth is created.[43]

---

43 For more information about these topics and more, please visit the Financial Consulate's Knowledge Center: https://financialconsulate.com/knowledge-center/

Chapter 5

The year 1995 began with Chris and I finally running our firm the way we'd always dreamed—as doctors of personal finance, working on a fee-only basis. The initial shift to fee-only cut our income by 50 percent, but it didn't take long to recover to previous levels. After Bev's retirement, Chris brought on an extremely organized woman named Nikki. We were as ready as we could be to face the end of the millennium.

Focusing on Relationships

In 1997, the global economy was rocked by the collapse of the ruble. International markets and small-cap stocks were especially affected, and our business began to decline. Chris and I met to discuss the future of our company, and as we spoke, we realized that we had been focusing more on money than on people.

Even on our radio show, called *A Wealth of Advice* and for which we used Pink Floyd's "Money" as the theme song, I'd adopted almost a Jim Cramer-ish bent, opining on individual stocks during each episode. This was both easy and fun for me, since following stocks and the markets was a passion, but again, it put our focus on money more than on people.

If you know anything about the Bible, you know that while money itself isn't evil, focusing on the love of money is. Chris and I turned to prayer and asked God what we should do. God sent a message saying we should quit the radio show. This was a difficult pill to swallow since much of our new business came from the radio show exposure. Despite that, His message was clear.

Leaving the radio was difficult, but it immediately brought people back into focus, and in 1998, the new purpose of our company showed itself: *to try and help lessen the worry and burden of money management so our clients have more time to spend building relationships.*

When we shared our new message, to my surprise, it truly resonated with people. Our clients were very receptive to the idea of using money and wealth to support emotional needs. Yet, business wasn't exactly booming. In the late 1990s tech stocks were trading at a hundred times earnings, whereas you'd expect them to be trading at twenty-five to fifty times earnings. Just about every dotcom stock was seen as potentially disruptive, yet most were illusions of a company with a .com after their name. We felt dotcoms were dangerous, so we had our clients investing primarily in value and dividend stocks, which we considered cheap to buy because no one wanted them.[44]

Of course, this also meant that an advisor with a strategy built around investing in these unpopular positions wasn't going to be too popular. We reached a ceiling with our assets under management, and we simply couldn't break through.

Still, I was at peace. I finally felt I was moving forward like a doctor of personal finance. Seeing money as nothing more than a **very good, neutral tool** and **refocusing on relationships as a priority** put me on a fulfilling track not just for myself, but for my clients. As for the doubt some had about my strategy of investing in value and dividend stocks

---

44 Please see disclaimer on page 4.

rather than internet stocks… well, my instincts were better understood once the dotcom bubble burst in early 2000.[45]

Divine Intervention

Being a financial advisor with a passion for the Lord not only helped keep my career in the proper perspective, it also brought me clients that were Divinely placed in my life. One such client was Beatrice.

Beatrice called in 2000. She had heard me on the radio and wanted me to come to her home and do her taxes. I was hesitant at first. I could tell from her voice that she was significantly older, and clients like Beatrice are often not very open to making changes about the way they do things. I didn't want to work on her tax return unless I could benefit her in some way, and if she wouldn't make changes, it was unlikely that I would. Still, I decided to meet with her.

The first thing I noticed was that her home, while certainly livable, was not in the best shape. It hadn't been maintained well over the years, and its age was showing. Beatrice, a woman of at least seventy-five but probably closer to eighty, greeted and invited me in. We spoke, and I learned that she'd never been married. She was independent and confident and clearly enjoyed her eccentric way of life.

One of her hobbies was to go through magazines and cut out photos that intrigued her. She would affix the photos to cardboard and begin to paint over the top with oil paints that matched the colors in the actual photograph. The end result was what appeared to be original oil paintings made on the most unlikely of canvases.

After we had spoken a bit, Beatrice pulled out her tax forms, including a 1099-DIV from a company paying her a dividend. The company was General Electric, which was paying about a 0.7 percent dividend at that time in 2000. Yet, the amount of the dividend she received was

---

45 Please see disclaimer on page 4.

$12,000. I was stunned but immediately began calculating what her GE stock holding had to be to create a $12,000 dividend. Quick math told me it was about $1.5 million worth of GE stock.

All told, her assets totaled about $1.8 million, and she was living on about $12,000 a year—which explained the lack of house maintenance.

I learned that she had never worked a day in her life. She had inherited the GE stock from her parents, causing resentment among her other siblings. Since she had never worked and never married, she had no Social Security benefit or Medicare. Just that GE dividend, and almost $2 million in assets behind it.

To my surprise, she was very receptive to the changes I thought she should make to the way her portfolio was structured. Once she was on board, I quickly got a lawyer to put together a charitable remainder trust (CRT).

Charitable Remainder Trust

A trust that holds a future donation for a charity made by a donor. Once the gift is placed into the trust, assets are sold and reinvested. The donor gets a present value charitable donation based on an annuity income for a certain term or life that is paid to the donor. At the end of the annuity term, the payments stop, and the trust is liquidated to the residual charity.

Because I felt that GE was grossly overvalued at the time and I wanted to sell it without creating a sizable capital gains tax, I thought the best option was to gift it to the CRT trust. This would also help in the event that she had medical bills, since assets in a CRT can't be attached by creditors. This was a very real concern since Beatrice had neither medical insurance nor Medicare.

Additionally, since a CRT pays out an income to the donor, it allowed us to create an income for Beatrice that could pay for living expenses for the rest of her life. In addition, we kept about $400,000 in cash in a high-yield savings account for emergencies.

After working with Beatrice for a while, I became curious about why she'd called us. It turns out that she was listening to a radio show we did in 1997 that happened to fall on Christmas Eve. During the show, my guest was a pastor, and we talked about how the greatest gift we could ever receive in our lives was Jesus. The show so moved her that three years later, when she wanted someone to do her tax returns, she remembered us and called.

We worked with Beatrice for a number of years. Once, she called to tell us that she was selling her home, which was valued at $65,000, to a guy who sent her a flyer and offered her $32,000 cash. Knowing that she had significant assets and a comfortable income from the CRT, I didn't try to talk her out of this. She asked me to take her to the settlement, and I agreed.

This was in 2000, before the housing bubble, a time when flipping houses was extremely popular. Attending the settlement with Beatrice and I was the financier and the flipper who would be doing the work to increase the value of the home after purchase. I could tell immediately that the financier was not someone who had the same definition of "wealth" as I did. He seemed like he lived his life to make more and more money. He and the flipper got into an argument, and the financier decided not to give the flipper the money to buy the house, right as we were all sitting there expecting to settle.

I knew that Beatrice wanted to be out of the house, and I wanted to see her living in a community setting that she could enjoy. I took the financial guy away from the table and tried to appeal to his better nature. "You see that lady over there?" I asked the financier. "She's eighty years old. She just wants $32,000 for the house. Just give the flipper the money so the woman can get on with her life."

The financier hesitated, then agreed that he would do it. But he made sure to say he was doing it for Beatrice, not for the flipper. Frankly, I didn't care who he did it for, I just wanted it done for my client. In the end, the flipper ended up selling the house for $80,000.

After the settlement, as I drove Beatrice home, we started talking about her past, and she told me a story. She said that when she was eighteen years old, at the end of twelfth grade, the priest of her Catholic school invited each of the students to come to the Catholic seminary to fast, pray, and be silent for two days. He said it would prove to be a blessing to them and that whatever they asked for during the vigil would come true for them. Only Beatrice and four others accepted the priest's offer.

She didn't eat and stayed in the seminary until the end. At the end of her story, Beatrice looked at me and said, "Do you know what I asked for?" I answered that I did not, and she said, "I asked that God send me somebody to take care of me when I'm an old lady and I'm all alone. I realize you are the answer to that prayer."

Beatrice may have been one of the few clients who knew that God was involved in our working relationship, but it comes as no surprise to me that He so obviously was. **There's no question that we have to be professional in all our relationships, but at the same time, there is a very personal nature to what we do.**

I learned to better balance the personal and the professional from Dr. Ben Carson when I read his book, *Gifted Hands*. In the book, Dr. Carson said that he was taught all through medical school to never get personally connected with his patients because when they die, it will burn you out, that he wouldn't be able to handle it. Dr. Carson went on to say that it was wrong. He said he should be personally invested with them so that he actually gets energized. That even when bad things happen, it may hurt for a while, but it actually taught him to be a better doctor.[46]

At our firm, we go with that same philosophy. If a client wants to be personal with us, we are going to be personal with them. Yet at the same time, if a client wants to keep a distance, we respect that and accept those boundaries.

Beatrice was not a client who wanted distance. So when she needed help moving out of her house and into an independent retirement community called Charlestown, we were right there to assist. Once she settled into her new home, two women from my staff, Nikki and DeAnna, took Beatrice under their wings, taking her to doctors' appointments and other places until Beatrice's death three years later.

There is a personal line that, ethically, I cannot cross, and Beatrice found that out when one day she told me she wanted to leave her estate to me. I was touched and felt a tremendous sense of peace that I'd been so helpful to her that she was inspired to make such a gesture. But I explained to her that I could not accept such a generous gift. She then asked if she could instead leave it to some of the employees in my office. Since those employees were not her advisor, there was no problem, and she set it up. Beatrice left a portion of her estate to Nikki and DeAnna and the rest went to charity.

Knowing Beatrice was a gift. Helping her in her later years was a blessing. I am also lucky enough to have a couple of her painted creations hanging in our office today, **a constant reminder of the beauty and humanity in every soul we encounter.**

---

46 Gifted Hands: The Ben Carson Story, paperback; February 10, 1992

Pension Problems

Beatrice wasn't the only notable client to come to us that year. Harvey, an employee with Baltimore Gas and Electric (before it was called Exelon), visited us when he was trying to decide between taking his pension payment as a monthly annuity or in a lump sum.

Going through his Financial Physical™, we saw that Harvey also had a 401(k) with BG&E, which was already a nice lump sum he could pull from. Based on that and his current and future financial needs, we advised Harvey to take his pension payment as a monthly annuity. Then, we would take his 401(k) and roll it over into an IRA. This not only gave him a tidy monthly income but allowed us to reduce his risks by properly diversifying the 401(k) sum.[47]

Often, when faced with a decision like this, people will be told by financial advisors that they need to take the lump sum because not only will their children then get whatever's unspent after they pass away, but they can invest that money and make a profit.

These points can be true and must be considered, but these are decisions that have to be thought out from a much more objective point of view. Economically biased people may encourage you to take the lump sum so they can invest it and earn fees and commissions.

Let's say a sixty-five-year-old is offered the choice between a lump sum of $500,000 and an annuity payment of $3,600 a month. At sixty-five, you can assume you'll get that payout for about twenty-five years. With the lump sum, you have the benefit of the liquidity, and it's something that your spouse or children can inherit if you pass away, which is not true of the monthly payout.

But on the negative side, there's no guarantee you will invest it in positions that gain in value. You also have no outside control measures ensuring you don't spend it too quickly. And what if you have a bad

47 Please see disclaimer on page 4.

accident and somebody sues you for $5 million, and you've got this lump sum?

While the annuity payout will only last over your lifetime, it is a guaranteed source of income that is safe from creditors. Although inflation can negatively impact the spending power of that income, there is no need to worry about investing it in a losing position or spending the total amount and being left with nothing. The right choice for each individual will vary and must be evaluated without the advisor's potential economic bias influencing the decision.

A couple years later, Harvey told us that while he'd chosen the monthly annuity, a lot of his coworkers had chosen the lump sum payout. After receiving the payouts, these former Exelon employees suffered through a three-year bear market from 2000 to 2002.

Advisors should be fiduciaries so that an objective overview of the option between lump sum versus annuity is discussed. No matter what someone is helping you with—insurance, investing, saving, or debt repayment—it is absolutely critical to be aware of their economic bias. You need to understand what is motivating them and how they make money on these transactions. Understanding this information will help you better assess whether the advisor is working in your best interests.

Becoming an Ambassador for Change

In June 2001, three months before the 9/11 attacks, I noticed something odd. The markets dipped for no discernible reason.[48] Later, after the 9/11 attack, when markets had been closed for a week, we learned that around March, Middle Eastern investors had purchased put options on the US market.[49] Since put options guarantee the buyer the option to

---

48 https://www.jstor.org/stable/10.1086/503645?seq=3

49 https://www.irishtimes.com/news/unusual-trading-before-attacks-investi-gated-1.397265

sell a position at a set price during a certain period, it is very likely that these options were purchased by investors who knew about the imminent attacks and anticipated a falling market as a result.

The lesson to take from this is that the movement of markets today is based on events that might not take place until the future. This can make it exceptionally hard for the average investor to intuit what daily market movements mean and to decide how to make decisions around them.

The 9/11 attacks had a profound effect on me, as they did the rest of the country. During this time, I wanted nothing more than real change to help people prepare and be proactive. I again wanted to build an organization that was bigger than me. I wanted to be sure that no matter what happened to me, clients would be cared for by colleagues who shared my core values and passion for our mission.

Around this time, I found an organization that could help me network with like-minded colleagues for real change. That organization was the National Association of Personal Financial Advisors (NAPFA). NAPFA was formed in 1983 by a group of advisors who wanted to serve clients without the potential bias of commissions impacting the relationship.[50] The 4,400 members of NAPFA are fee-only advisors held to a fiduciary standard and committed to aligning their recommendations solely to their clients' interests.

According to the NAPFA site, their member advisors live by the following three values:

> - To be the beacon for independent, objective financial advice for individuals and families
> - To be the champion of financial services delivered in the public interest

---

50 https://www.napfa.org/about-us

> - To be the standard bearer for the emerging profession of financial planning

Joining NAPFA was one of the best moves I ever made. The difference in the NAPFA advisor moral code was immediately apparent from my very first meeting, during which I saw members arguing with industry wholesalers who were there to suggest a particular product. The NAPFA members argued with the wholesalers about the merits of the product, as they didn't see how it would benefit clients.

This was vastly different from the interactions between wholesalers and advisors that I was used to seeing at broker-dealer-hosted conferences where an adversarial stance taking the side of the clients was not the norm. NAPFA members were passionate about how to make money for the client as opposed to what I was used to seeing in the industry—a focus on how the advisors could make money.

NAPFA helped me fully flesh out my approach to advising clients so that I could develop into the advisor I wanted to be. Working with Schwab and NAPFA were pieces that helped me complete the metamorphosis from sales associate to an advisor who approaches planning like a doctor of personal finance, ultimately becoming that ambassador for change I had long envisioned.

Can Your Advisor Do This?

There are several requirements for me to be a financial advisor who operates as an ambassador for change. First, I have to be completely independent. When an advisor is affiliated with a brokerage firm, bank, or insurance company, they are not a true financial advisor because they are representing the company, not the client. This does not make the advisor evil or bad, but it can mean that the clients they serve are not getting the benefit of someone with in-depth knowledge about a wide range of products, strategies, and facets of financial life.

These advisors are not trained to be doctors of personal finance, but instead profit generators for themselves and the company they represent. The culture is not designed to be in the best interests of the client.

As I've said before, an advisor affiliated with a brokerage firm, insurer, or bank is like a doctor working for a drug company. Can you imagine having a doctor who works for Pfizer? You might love working with him, but you would be completely correct to question whether it's right of him to prescribe Pfizer medications and to do so as soon as they come out, rather than testing that you need them. You may think you can completely trust him, but you should be concerned about whether other pharmaceutical company drugs might better serve your needs, offer fewer side effects, or have better overall results.

Over the years, I have seen countless clients who have really bonded with and liked their advisor, but were not getting the guidance and wisdom they needed. Sometimes the advisor in question is a friend or family member, which adds an extra layer of difficulty.

Recently, we signed a new client, Mike, whose broker was a friend with a Wall Street firm. Mike is worth about $14 million, and he earns about $3 million a year.

Mike's friend, and their planning team, chose commission-based Virginia 529 plans for Mike's kids. Seems harmless, until you realize that they could have put those funds in the commission-free Maryland 529 plan, and Mike would've gotten a tax deduction and would've had a far better 529 plan.

Another questionable choice they made was to set up IRAs for him. Mike's profession exposed him to personal liability suits, which means he should not have any IRA money. His retirement savings should all be in a 401(k), which has the strongest liability protection. The broker managed the 401(k), so they definitely knew he had one.

Mike's broker also set up a cash balance plan for him, which is a type of tax-deferred retirement plan. This might have made sense five or more years ago, but it no longer suited Mike's needs since he had accumulated excessive pretax funds in a potentially taxable estate.

I consider estate taxes to be the evilest of all government taxes. These egregious taxes hurt the little guy who does not have a legion of lawyers to help. Currently, the federal estate exemption is $12,060,000, but in 2026, the estate tax exemption returns to approximately $6,500,000.[51] There is portability in the exemptions, so if one spouse dies and does not use any exemption, then the surviving spouse inherits their exemption, essentially doubling it. Unfortunately, this portability is only true if you file an estate tax return.

There are also twelve states and the District of Columbia with an estate tax with exemptions ranging from $1 million to $12 million. Only a few of those states, such as Maryland, recognize portability.

Let's look at how this might work. Let's say a Maryland man dies in 2022 with an estate of $4 million, all passing to his wife. There's no need for probate, and because their estate is less than $6.5 million, no one is concerned about federal portability.

Ten years later, the wife dies, and her estate has grown to $7 million. Maryland's exemption is only $5 million with no cost-of-living adjustment, which means the wife's estate is subject to 16 percent of the $2 million over $5 million for a state tax of $320,000. This would have been ZERO if someone filed an estate tax return in Maryland for her when her husband died because the Maryland portability would have given her an extra $5 million exemption for a total $10 million exemption.

---

51 https://www.irs.gov/newsroom/estate-and-gift-tax-faqs

We file these portability returns frequently for our clients, just in case. I already have five clients whose heirs will see a significant benefit because we preemptively filed these returns.

The New York estate tax is even more absurd because if someone dies in 2022 with an estate worth $6.15 million, they may owe NY $125,000. But if the client dies with exactly $6 million, then they owe zero. The reason is NY has a cliff estate tax for anyone whose estate is greater than $6.11 million in 2022. There is no portability in NY. Many good NY estate attorneys will write in a charity clause that allows the executor to donate estate assets to a charity, reducing the estate just enough to avoid the cliff.

Too often these small millionaire clients have no idea the snares that stand ready to capture them and their family due to overt complexity. Dealing with personal financial advisors who are not trained as doctors of comprehensive advice certainly doesn't help.

Back to our client Mike. The first thing we helped him do was to get into the Maryland 529 plan. As a fee-only fiduciary advisor, I knew that the move to the 529 was best for the client since it eliminated fees and commissions.

Next up was the IRA money. We took $76,000 in nondeductible money and shifted it into a Roth IRA, then moved the rest into his 401(k). Of course, we did this only after reducing the costly fees the 401(k) was littered with.

Together, he and his wife will end up with $152,000 in a Roth, tax-free. The rest of his money is protected in the 401(k) plan for liability purposes. The IRA to 401(k) transfer represented another $500,000 that our firm will not be actively managing.

All told, of the $14 million that the Wall Street advisors invested and made 1 percent plus on, our firm will end up only investing about $8 million, and we will make maybe 0.8 percent. Even after only charging a management fee on half the money they did, and a smaller management fee at that, we still make a great living while Mike benefits from these income tax and estate-efficient moves.

Working with a big-name firm doesn't mean you're getting the benefit of some secret expertise. Often, the advisors at these firms are limited in their knowledge and in what products they can recommend, which puts your personal financial management at a disadvantage. Sadly, this means these professionals are far from being "financial advisors." They actually are investment salespeople.

A professional advisor should be able to walk you through complicated tax strategies and estate planning options that put your needs and benefits at the center. They should be able to help you with an in-depth review of insurance policies and make recommendations for true risk-management plans. They should be able to help you with elder care and college planning, even if it means bringing in other professionals and helping oversee and explain to you what those other professionals are recommending.

The Power of Prophecy

God has never been shy about sending me messages, although it sometimes takes me a little while to understand them. In 2001, after attending a church meeting in North Carolina, I was invited to meet with some church members who wanted to prophecy to me about a message the Lord had for me at that time in my life. My wife and I went, and one of the prophesying members looked at me and said, "The Lord intends to give you gold." He then said, "I think that gold is wisdom," but when he said it, I immediately had a sense it was some form of financial blessing.

About a day or two later, I received a call from a brokerage firm out of the Midwest. On the phone was the firm's general counsel asking to buy the trademark for our newsletter and our old radio show, *A Wealth of Advice*. Since we'd ended the show, we were only using the name for our newsletter, so I had no problem selling it. The general counsel offered me a not insignificant sum of money, and I said I'd think about it.

Later, as I prayed about it, I realized this was the gold that had been prophesied in North Carolina. I was moved by the feeling that I should ask for more than what I was offered, so when I called them back, I asked them to double their offer. A few weeks later, the check for the amount I'd requested was sent.

God has always been a central figure in my life, but His messages aren't always easy for me to hear. In 2006, after moving to a new home overlooking Liberty reservoir in Maryland, Bev and I discovered that the property needed some work. One of the worst aspects of the home was its kitchen. I love to cook, so a dingy, poorly planned kitchen was not going to satisfy me, and we decided our first project would be to renovate the large room.

As I searched for contractors, a friend of mine recommended a contractor named Kelly. Up until this time, my thought process had always been to get a project done for the least amount of money possible without sacrificing quality. After talking to a few other builders, I met with Kelly, and his quote was outside what I wanted to spend. I wanted to look for someone cheaper, but I could feel a pull from the Lord, basically telling me that I was not supposed to worry about getting the cheapest price, but to hire whomever the Lord wanted—and He wanted me to hire Kelly.

Kelly began work on the project soon after, bringing two workers with him—his eighteen-year-old son Matt and his son's friend Robbie. The kitchen turned out amazing, exceeding my wildest hopes. Kelly's craftsmanship was so good, Bev and I decided to ask him to work on other projects as necessary.

Kelly's son Matt was an unbelievably hard worker. In addition to working with his dad, he also was a volunteer firefighter and did landscaping and snow removal. In 2010, Maryland got more than fifty inches of snow over a five-day period. For two weeks, Matt worked endlessly, clearing his clients' driveways. A few weeks later, he contracted spinal meningitis. After being misdiagnosed, Matt's health worsened, and he ended up in the hospital, but it was too late. The spinal meningitis had already taken such a strong foothold, there was no hope for recovery, and he passed away.

I went to the hospital as soon as I heard Matt was sick, but sadly, I was not able to get there before he died. I gave as much comfort to Kelly and his wife, also named Beverly, as I could, praying together as we processed their son's passing.

A couple days later, Kelly called and asked me to be the pastor at his son's funeral. I had done one or two baptisms in the past and had spoken at a couple of funerals, but Kelly didn't know that, so I wasn't sure what made him ask me. He said that when we'd prayed together at the hospital, he felt the Holy Spirit—a feeling he'd had only once before, as a young boy in church. He also said that if they were going to have a funeral for Matt, they didn't want just some preacher up there talking. They wanted someone who knew Matt.

I agreed to be the pastor at the funeral, but when I hung up the phone, I spoke to the Lord and told Him what a difficult position He'd put me in. Kelly and his wife had just lost their only son—a boy who was with his father all the time, as a colleague, employee, hunting partner, and so much more. Once I'd expressed myself, I made a request to God about the funeral, which was to be in Pennsylvania. I said, "Just make it a beautiful day. That's all I ask for."

On the morning of the funeral, I pulled up my weather app to see a giant rainstorm bearing down on this region of Pennsylvania. There was no doubt there would be a torrential downpour during the service.

To say I was frustrated is putting it mildly. Once again, I spoke to God and said, "I asked for one thing. I asked for a beautiful day, and look at this storm." A thought crossed my mind then that I should read chapter 38 of the book of Job. The very first line of that chapter in the version I was reading is, "Out of the storm, the Lord spoke…"

When I read that verse, I understood. While I might have wanted good weather, it would be through this storm that the Lord would speak to all those mourning Matt as he was laid to rest. My message was, "I cannot tell you why, but I can tell you who Matt is and who my God is."

Ten years later, Kelly's wife Bev passed away, and I was again asked to be the pastor at her funeral. Now, more than fifteen years after meeting, Kelly and I still talk several early mornings each week. I am so grateful that even though I didn't understand God's plan from the beginning, He wove Kelly and his family into my life and my heart.

Tools for Financial Planning

In this chapter, I talked about the investing ups and downs of the dotcom bubble and the 9/11 attacks. I also introduced you to Beatrice, Harvey, and Mike, clients who had planning needs that we were able to satisfy, thanks to our client-focused approach.

To close out the chapter, I want to talk to you about why giving more to charity matters to your financial plan. I then want to explain why having a Roth IRA strategy is so vital to your retirement planning and also talk about how different it is to invest in disruption today than it was in 1999.

- Give more, have more
- Everyone needs a Roth strategy
- Investing in disruption

Give More, Have More

At the same time I was preparing notes for this chapter in the book, I was getting ready to record our Thanksgiving charity show. I have always believed that the more you give, the more you have. Finances flow in and out of our lives with an energy like that of a river's current. Over the course of my life, I have seen that when you give, that river flows, allowing you to better enjoy the wealth you have. By being charitable, you increase satisfaction and contentment.

Sadly, I have also seen that when you're not generous, you become more of a cistern, accumulating water that eventually stagnates and may get polluted.

When you encourage the flow of your financial river by constantly giving and receiving, you bring this life force into your net worth. Charitable giving is a critical source of outflow from your river. Not an enforced type of giving, like a begrudging tithe you feel you must relinquish, but with a generosity that flows out of your heart.

Those who have this innate desire to give tend to be wealthier because they're very content with what they have and they feel they have more than enough to help others in need.

Ways to Be Charitable

There are endless ways you can be charitable each and every day of your life. It's not just about donating to charities but also about helping a neighbor, fellow parishioner, a colleague, or even strangers who are having a tough time. It could mean giving money to a beggar on the street without judging what they will do with it or donating to a project to improve a community in need. However you choose to do it, giving to someone in need creates a positive, life-sustaining moment.

One of the ways we help our clients facilitate charitable giving is through qualified charitable distributions from an IRA, appreciated assets to a donor-advised fund, a private charitable trust to create your own charity, or with a charitable remainder trust like we set up for Beatrice.

Never give for tax benefits, but only from a heart overflowing with thankfulness and a desire to help. If your heart desires to give, then a personal financial advisor should be able to develop the strategy to maximize the tax benefits to enhance the overall gift.

In the old days, when the standardized deduction was lower, itemization was more common. During that time, those making charitable donations and itemizing would get a deduction for every dollar of their charitable giving. Today, because the standard deduction is so high and the state tax deduction is limited to $10,000, it takes a larger amount to begin to see a difference on the tax return as a result of charitable giving.

One workaround for this is a donor-advised fund. A client who gives money to charity each year but sees very little tax benefit can give five years' worth of donations all at once, with a highly appreciated security, by putting the asset into a donor-advised fund.[52] The year they deposit the funds, they get a deduction for the full market value and never pay taxes on the gain. They get a full deduction in the year of gift but can make donations to their chosen charities over the next five years or more.

For older clients who are charitably inclined, another option is to do qualified charitable distributions from their IRA. Once you've reached age 70.5, you can take up to $100,000 per year of your traditional IRA and give it to charity without reporting it on your tax return.[53] This transaction also counts against the required minimum distribution (RMD) criteria, and you can choose what charitable organizations receive the donations.

---

52 https://www.schwabcharitable.org/maximize-your-impact/tax-strategies
53 https://www.kitces.com/blog/qualified-charitable-distribution-qcd-from-ira-to-satisfy-rmd-rules-and-requirements/

Sadly, too often advisors don't recommend these strategies to their charitably minded clients because they require more administrative work. But having a tax-advantage charitable giving strategy is what you pay an advisor to help develop. Make sure your advisor does not work as little as possible and try to make as much as possible at your expense.

Everyone Needs a Roth Strategy

Everyone needs to accumulate as much as possible in Roth IRAs or Roth 401(k)s. The reason for this is simple: everyone needs tax-free money, especially when they head into retirement, because the tax laws are full of tax landmines. Some of those landmines are also so far out of date as to be harmful to today's finances.

For example, did you know that the dollar limits determining how much income you can have before your Social Security is taxable were set back in 1982 and haven't changed since? In 1982, a single person making over $25,000 had to begin paying taxes on up to 50 or 85 percent of their Social Security income.[54] In 2022, it's the same amount—even though $25,000 in 1982 is equivalent to about $75,000 today. This traps seniors today in webs created over forty years ago.

But when income is distributed from a Roth, it doesn't impact adjusted gross income triggering Social Security taxability. In fact, if a retiree could take $100,000 a year from a Roth for the rest of their life, then they would never pay a nickel in tax on their Social Security income.

It's important to understand all the different traps laid for seniors taking Social Security and Medicare so you can develop strategies to deal with them. Traps like Medicare's income-related monthly adjustment amount (IRMAA), which requires singles making more than $91,000 or married $182,000 per year (2022 figures) to pay a surcharge tax on their

---

54 https://www.ssa.gov/policy/docs/issuepapers/ip2015-02.html

Medicare Part B and Medicare Part D premiums.[55] Even if you earn just $1 more than $91,000/$182,000, you're on the hook for added taxes. This, again, is why getting income from a tax-free Roth is a vital strategy.

None of this means you should just throw all your IRA or 401(k) contributions at Roth plans. There is a reason this section calls for a Roth *strategy*. A Roth is the best way to counteract certain tax pitfalls after retirement, but there are times you want to contribute to a pretax, traditional IRA or 401(k). Those who are in their forties or fifties and living in a high-tax state but planning to move to a lower-tax state can be better served getting the tax deduction on contributions. It also benefits those whose income is around $180,000 or more with a child going to college. They need their income to fall below $160,000 to get the $2,500 American Opportunity Tax credit.

Regardless, it's a good idea to at least open and minimally fund a Roth IRA as early as possible. Roth distributions become totally tax-free after you have two things happen:

1. You turn 59.5

2. You've had a Roth outstanding for more than five years

It sounds simple enough, but five years is a complicated concept because it's based not on the actual date the Roth is opened but on the effective tax year it is opened. Let's say, on April 14, 2023, you opened and funded a Roth IRA *for the 2022 tax year*. Then your five-year rule would end January 1, 2027. But if you open the Roth IRA on April 20, 2023, for the 2023 tax year, it won't end until January 1, 2028.

By opening a Roth as soon as possible, you get that five-year clock ticking so the Roth distributions can be tax-free as soon as you need them after turning age 59.5. Roth 401(k) balances at any age should be rolled to a Roth IRA when leaving an employer, except if you have a greater

---

55 https://secure.ssa.gov/poms.nsf/lnx/0601101020

than normal liability risk in your profession. Getting past the five-year rule can make a Roth IRA rollover from your 401(k) far more flexible. (Note: Traditional IRA money should normally be rolled to your new employer plan.)

There's no such thing as a simple strategy. You've got to think it out, consider your tax bracket and your tax thresholds, consider where you live and where you will retire, and so forth to create an effective Roth strategy.

Investing in Disruption

One of the differences between now and the build-up to the dotcom bubble bursting is the speed with which technology is accelerating and how our "normal" way of life is being disrupted. Before the dotcom bubble, disruptions such as air travel, cars, and even television took decades to develop and take hold of society.

Accelerations today are far more advanced and happen with a rapidity few can keep up with. Look at cell phone technology. In 1983, Motorola released the first commercially sold handheld mobile phone.[56] It took about twenty-five years before cell phones were ubiquitous. After that point, it only took a few years for the development of flip phones, tablets, and smartphones to replace the original cell phones.[57]

And that's just one example. The past fifteen years have seen tremendous change in how we handle document processing and storage, online banking, and investing while also bringing us new types of currencies, video meetings, and more.

In our daily lives, these technological advances are embraced and give us more time, more autonomy, and more options. But when it comes to deciding which ones are worth investing in, it's difficult for anyone to

56 https://en.wikipedia.org/wiki/Mobile_phone
57 https://parade.com/5457/iraphael/the-evolution-of-the-cell-phone/

analyze which disruptions and so-called "disruptor" companies will stay, and which will go the way of Quibi and eToys. It's also difficult to see which ones might be nothing more than empty promises, like Theranos.

During the dotcom boom, internet-related companies were highly valued, almost without regard to their realistic potential for success. With no ability to judge the performance history of new start-ups with rapidly developed, disruptive models, many investors and advisors alike got caught in the hype.

Today, many compare high-flying disruptor companies to the dotcom companies of 2000, but nothing could be further from the truth. The dotcoms were not innovative, just a new retail system. Today's disruptors are real companies with real innovation in automobiles, medicine, the digital world, currencies, robots, energy, and more. They will be quite volatile, but most will endure.[58]

---

58 For more information about these topics and more, please visit the Financial Consulate's Knowledge Center: https://financialconsulate.com/knowledge-center/

Chapter 6

By 2003 the dotcom boom had gone bust as many of these highly overvalued dotcom companies finished spending all the venture capital they'd collected and then shuttered their sites. Our clients, who may have doubted our strategy of investing in value and dividend stocks during the rise of the dotcoms, were grateful we had done so.

At this time, Chris had been promoted to head of operations, but it was time for him to answer a higher calling. He had finished training to become a pastor and was finally ready to commit to his church, ultimately leaving our firm.

Shortly after he left CAPCO, we decided to come up with a new name. We brainstormed and tried many options, but none of them were right. One night, I was having dinner with a pastor I'd met several years before. He had no idea we were searching for a new name, yet at dinner he looked at me and said, "You're an ambassador to the financial community on earth from the Kingdom of Heaven, and your company is a financial consulate." Finally, we had a name: Financial Consulate.

When we designed our logo, we used the name as inspiration and based it on a reimagining of Dupont circle in Washington, where many embassies are.

The loss of Chris left us an advisor spot to fill, and Nikki decided to take the CFP' exam. We also hired a young man named Ron to handle trading. Ron learned quickly and became our investment trader. As the firm continued to grow, I needed an operating and compliance officer, so I approached Chris's brother-in-law, Bob, who was working for a broker-dealer. He expressed interest in taking on the position with our firm.

Things were progressing very well until early 2005, when Nikki and Ron needed to leave the firm without notice. This left us severely understaffed, so both Bev and Chris returned on a temporary basis. While Bev went back to her former role, Chris focused on training new additions, one of whom was Chuck Bender, who has gone on to become our current CFO.

Back in 2003, Chuck had heard me on the radio and decided to reach out. He wrote to me and said that he was interested in the industry and wanted my input on how to get to know the more about it. I took him out to dinner, and I told him we'd stay in touch. A Virginia Tech Hokie, Chuck worked for Ernst & Young out of college and then moved to McCormick & Company. From there, he went on to be CFO of a start-up, but he wasn't yet satisfied.

When our business needed help in 2005, Chuck was one of the first people who came to mind. I wrote to him and asked if he would be interested in joining the Financial Consulate. He decided to work part time with us to try it out and within a month decided to go full time.

The mix of our staff, our values, our approach, and the customer-first focus of Schwab was a winning combination. One of the reasons we appreciate Schwab so much is that they are very big on business development for their independent registered investment advisors. As part of this push to develop our business, they asked us to create a reference list of our core values and mission statement. We took this to heart and refined our six core values.

Six Core Values

When you visit our website, you will see the following core values and brief descriptions:

- **Integrity**
  We are honest and fair, cognizant of our propensity to exhibit bias, always working to eliminate it.

- **Competency**
  We are credentialed, educated, experienced, and committed to perpetual self-improvement.

- **Collaboration**
  We work with each other, external specialists, colleagues, and clients for our edification and optimal outcomes for our clients.

- **Innovation**
  We anticipate the future in the present, persistently questioning and innovating in our roles and as a company.

- **Freedom**
  We foster an environment in which clients and employees are free to come and free to go, welcoming into the fold and blessing those who move on.

- **Love**
  We nurture, protect, and cherish, without expectation.

The list likely contains some values you expected to see and others you didn't. The first four—integrity, competency, collaboration and innovation—are easy to understand. We want to be as honest and straightforward as we can possibly be, keeping our economic biases down. We continue to keep our skills up by studying, reading, watching, attending seminars, completing continuing education, and so on. We work together with other professionals and colleagues to bring the best we can to the client. We constantly innovate and look into new technology and strategies to be the best we can.

The last two values, freedom and love, are principles you don't normally see financial advisory firms embracing, and I'd like to take this opportunity to tell you our thought process around each of them.

A Deeper Look at Freedom and Love

Freedom means that if a client no longer wants to work with us, we are as gracious and professional at allowing them to transition to another firm as we are when we got them to join our firm. Our philosophy is, if we told our general practitioner that we wanted to begin working with a different doctor, we'd want them to be professional and helpful about it. We would want the same of our lawyer, accountant, and other professionals. What we don't want, and imagine our clients don't want either, is to be shamed or brow-beaten or have to argue for our information to be forwarded to a new provider.

We believe our clients should be free to come and free to go anytime, with the same blessings whether they are coming or going. When a client does decide to leave us, we try to keep their costs as low as possible and do our best to ensure that every asset we hold is transferable to any firm they want to move the assets to.

Here is what we mean by *love* in our values:

An unconditional choice to protect and nourish somebody without conditions placed around what they have to do.

In other words, if I choose to love someone, then it is not an emotion that simply arises from a feeling; it's a choice. When love is given by choice, it is unconditional. If the person who gives the love receives nothing in return, it is irrelevant.

In some ways, the values of freedom and love are a true representation of the Richard Bach quote that upended my last serious relationship before I met Bev: "If you love something, set it free. If it comes back, it's yours. If it doesn't, it never was."[59]

As part of our unconditional love for clients and the nurturing, care, and protection we offer them, we also let them know that if they want to leave us at any time, they can and it's not going to cost them extra fees or penalties. We're not going to do anything to manipulate them to stay. Those clients who really appreciate what we're doing are more than content to stay, and we're happier because we only have clients who want to be with us. As a result of our sincerely held values and mission statement, we score remarkable numbers on our client satisfaction surveys.

The freedom in our values isn't just for clients. It also extends to how we treat employees, as one of our former employees, Chris Pratt, can attest. It sounds counterintuitive, but the more open-handed you are with your children, your employees, your spouse, friends, and loved ones, the greater your relationships will become, despite the occasional pain you'll experience.

Chris was hired in 2005, a bright young guy fresh out of college. A fast learner, Chris was a great help after losing Nikki and Ron. But around his third or fourth year with the company, after we helped him get his licenses and CFP® credential, I could see that he had no passion for what he was doing.

Throughout my career, I was never just looking for employees to be warm bodies to help me make a lot of money and grow a business. I always saw employees as people who had been placed in my life so I

59 https://www.goodreads.com/quotes/574192-if-you-love-something-set-it-free-if-it-comes

could help them figure out their destiny, even if it didn't align with my own. Because ultimately, I don't believe that our job is to try to soak the most out of each employee for our benefit. Our job is to help them find and understand their calling in life.

Once I realized that Chris didn't have a passion for the industry and what he was doing, I talked to him about it. He admitted that he liked his work, but that it wasn't his calling. I advised Chris to go out there and find his passion and purpose and not just hang out in an industry because it was convenient. I then told him that we would help him for a short period while he tried whatever he wanted to try.

Soon after I told him that, Chris went on a three-month scuba diving research crew to Madagascar to study the coral reef. When he returned, he said he liked it, but wanted to go scuba diving in Guatemala and teach English as a second language. After doing that, he spent many years in South America teaching English as a second language and getting involved with the government.

By 2018 or so, Chris had returned to the US and, in an interesting turn of events, was working in his cousin's financial advisory firm. Sadly, just a few weeks before I was putting together this chapter, Chris's cousin passed away, leaving the business in Chris's hands in 2022. He reached out to us, and we gave him support and advice, and he seems to be doing well. We are happy to see him staying in touch with people he trusts and are glad we can be a part of his success story.

The world twists and turns, and it's impossible to say where you will be fifteen years from now. I'm glad that we have embraced freedom as a value, in part because I can see how important it was for Chris to get those years of freedom to become the man he is today. With our current employees, we uphold the same values.

Getting the Word Out

People have to know about you to want to do business with you, so in 2007 we hired a public relations person named Ben Lewis. He was excellent and really had connections all over. It was at this time when we started writing articles for *The Wall Street Journal*, Kiplinger, and *Money Magazine*. We also did television appearances here and there. One of the most important activities during this time was an exposé I did with Bloomberg on AARP.[60]

AARP positions itself as the guardian of seniors. As a fee-only, independent advisor, it is my duty to check out the different insurance offerings by AARP—because if they are good for my clients, then I will recommend them. As I looked into the coverage offered by the group, I was shocked because not only was it not better than other policies widely available, it was positively egregious.

I realized that I had only seen the tip of the iceberg and decided to dig deeper. I did a market analysis, comparing AARP products and pricing against others in the market, and I found that AARP had products that were far costlier than comparable products available in the wider market. Why? Because, in my opinion, the organization's profit motive was its priority.

After I was quoted in the press talking about this issue and my findings, Bloomberg Television came to our offices and taped a five-hour show with me. They validated my findings with other sources and went live with the segment. I monitor AARP insurance products, and to this day see no change and wonder why seniors would belong to this organization.

---

60 https://www.bloomberg.com/news/articles/2008-02-13/sure-its-from-aarp-dot-but-is-it-a-good-deal

Resurrecting the Radio Show

By 2007 the business had grown and we were operating it exactly as we wanted to—as fee-only advisors with a broker-dealer that supported a customer-first focus. We had established our core values and mission statement. But there was something missing. That something was revealed to me when Baltimore radio show host Sean Casey called me one morning and asked me to bring our show back to the airwaves.

"I told the station that I think we should have you back," Sean said during his totally out-of-the-blue call. It was truly miraculous. We had heeded God's message to end a radio show that consistently brought us new clients, refocused our language and approach to prioritize relationships, and now He wanted us back on the radio. Not only that, but Sean said the only spot they had available was Wednesday nights at 6:00 p.m., which was the exact night the radio show had been on before.

Of course, the old radio show title, *A Wealth of Advice*, and the old theme song, Pink Floyd's "Money," no longer fit our refocus. God's hand was steering this ship, so I decided to look to the Bible for inspiration on a new name. As a financial advisor who has read the Bible every year since 1995, I am especially interested in the financial terms it holds. I decided to research the Hebrew derivative of the words and scripture for money, riches, and wealth—terms that typically denote what we think about in the financial industry.

When I researched the first one—*money*—I learned that it actually has a derivative in greed, in other words, *idolatry*, which is when you believe there's a power that will give you the things you want in your life. I thought that was interesting because in the book of Galatians, Paul says that the love of money is idolatry. So people assume money has that kind of power, and yet money isn't powerful at all.

Money can't buy love. It can't save your life in the end. Even if you offer $1 billion to people with unswayable values and principles, you can't get them to do what you want if it goes against those personal truths.

Next I looked into the word *riches*. It comes from a derivative of pretending to be rich, to put all your effort into becoming rich. Riches are important to you; it's a lifelong goal to become rich.

Finally, with the word *wealth*, there was a derivative that meant contentment, satisfaction—almost like the word *wealth* meant when you become content in this much wealth, you'll find the greatest joy. But if you strive, if you lift money up as idolatry, if you strive to get rich, no matter how rich you get, no matter how much money you have, you'll always be dissatisfied. You'll always be looking for more money and more riches because you are not in the place of contentment and satisfaction.

After researching, I decided that this trifecta of terms for money—each of them with its own twist—was the ideal name for a show that was meant to help people learn how to put relationships first, enjoy their wealth, and keep money in its place. So we called our show, *Money, Riches, and Wealth* and used The Beatles' "Can't Buy Me Love" as the theme song.

When we got back to the studio mics, I didn't pick back up where I left off, with that Jim Cramer approach to pontificating about stocks. Instead, we talked about tax planning ideas, estate planning ideas, elder care issues, Social Security/Medicare planning, and strategies for helping kids with college tuition. We kept our show's topics centered around giving people advice to, as our mission statement says, **help them lessen the worry and burden of money management so they can focus on the true power of life, which is relationships.**

I believe one of the most important values delivered by our revamped radio show was that it gave us a perfect means of correcting the misperceptions people have about retirement planning, estate planning, and Medicare planning. I can't tell you how many times I hear people reiterate bad advice they got from a friend or colleague or how often I've seen people assume that advice thrown at them during a golf game must be true. So often, simple concepts get completely misunderstood and repeated over and over.

One of the most often repeated bits of misunderstood information is about Medicare. It's the idea that you have to sign up for Medicare Part B as soon as you turn sixty-five or you'll be penalized. The truth is, if you work with a company with twenty or more employees, and have medical insurance through that company, you don't have to sign up for Medicare Part B. You get a special enrollment period when you stop working, even if that doesn't happen until you're eighty years of age, and you can sign up for Medicare Part B without penalty.

Another Medicare myth we often have to dispel is the idea that with Medicare A, since you've already paid for it all your life, you might as well sign up for it at sixty-five years of age. But if you have a medical plan with an HSA (health savings account), signing up for Medicare Part A will immediately negate the ability to have an HSA, a topic I covered in more detail in Chapter 3.

Social Security is yet another topic we often cover on the show. People think that the best option is to begin taking their benefit as soon as possible. For a married couple, our general rule of thumb is the lowest earner takes benefits at full retirement age and the highest earner waits to age 70. If your spouse and you have a normal life expectancy, this tends to be the best statistical bet.

Letting the higher earner's benefits accumulate an additional 8 percent per year until they reach age seventy and then begin taking payments also assures the lower-earning spouse will receive these same maximum benefits adjusted to cost of living as the survivor.

Answered Prayers

It wasn't long after our radio show restarted that we got a call from an elderly woman named Lillian. She had purchased an annuity from a life insurance agent disguised as a bank manager. There are a lot of stockbrokers and life insurance agents disguised as bank managers, luring unsuspecting depositors into insurance or investment purchases. Lillian called because after making the purchase, she wisely began to doubt whether it was the right move to have made.

My associate Tim Maurer and I made the drive to see her, and that is when we got the full story. She'd had a $100,000 CD that had matured at her bank. Upon maturity, the bank manager convinced her to use the funds to buy an annuity. She had just received the paperwork and was still in her ten-day free look period when we arrived.

Sadly, it was as she'd expected. The annuity had not been a good choice. After reviewing the documents, I saw that the annuity had a ten-year deferred sales charge of 10 percent. At Lillian's age of eighty-eight, having a ten-year period where you can't surrender the contract without a penalty makes no sense.

Lillian had about six days left to cancel the annuity, so we needed to move quickly. Because I was already booked the next day, Tim decided to accompany Lillian to the bank to get her out of the ill-suited annuity product. It was a good thing he was there, because the bank manager was not about to let it go without a fight.

Still, Lillian was a tough little bird. She stuck to her guns, and the bank manager refunded her money. Once this was done, she told us that she wanted us to help her with her finances.

It was at this point when we finally came to realize just how alone Lillian was. Her brother, a major league baseball player who'd played with Babe Ruth, was fatally hit in the throat by a ball during spring training. Her husband died of Lou Gehrig's disease. Then Lillian's brother-in-law and niece died. Lillian's sister moved in with her, but then she passed away, too, leaving Lillian truly alone.

Far from being beaten by the challenges life had thrown at her, Lillian was pretty active. A devout woman, she prayed daily and mentioned to me that she always ended her prayers by praying for Jerusalem. She worked in a law firm throughout her early eighties. She also liked to do her own tax returns, using pencil and paper to complete the worksheets—a task that, upon review, I realized she had executed perfectly.

We began to compile a list of her assets, a mission that was easier said than done. She had about fifteen different bank accounts, many portfolios, and other assets scattered around. All told, she was worth about $2.5 million. But you wouldn't know that from the way she lived.

Her house was in a difficult neighborhood in Baltimore. She was concerned about break-ins, so she had nailed every window shut. The doors, too, were nailed shut, except for the back door. During the hot, humid Baltimore summer, temperatures inside her house would soar to more than one hundred degrees.

She had a 1960s gas oven that hadn't worked in years, so for food she would buy a single aluminum-foil-wrapped chicken wing at a local convenience store, bring it home, and place it on the pilot light to heat it up.

One day, I was at her home and she told me she had some Series E bonds. I asked her how many she had and instead of answering, she pulled back the floor-to-ceiling curtains in her living room, and there sat enormous stacks of bonds. Approximately $335,000 worth. Certainly enough to repair the stove and buy an air conditioner.

It was strange how similar Lillian was to Beatrice. Both living uncomfortably—and unreasonably—below their means during their twilight years. Realizing that this way of life wasn't healthy or safe for Lillian, I spoke to her about moving to a lovely community setting on the other side of town called Oakcrest.

At first, she was concerned she couldn't afford it. She had what I refer to as a *poverty spirit*. With close to $3 million in assets, she definitely could afford the move. But when you have the poverty spirit, you have an overriding sense that you are poor, no matter what your net worth says.

Once I showed her the numbers and assured her she could afford it, her next concern was that she needed a three-bedroom unit. I knew the chances of this happening soon were slim, and I told her that this might mean she had to wait years for a unit to become available, especially since there was already a waiting list in place. She was adamant that it had to be three bedrooms.

We put her on the list at Oakcrest, and we were all prepared for a long wait. Then one day when I was leaving her house, I remembered her comment about praying for Jerusalem every night. It hit me that there's a scripture verse that says God will bless those who pray for the peace of Jerusalem.[61] I decided to speak to God, and said, "Lord, you say it right here. You say that you'll bless those who pray for the peace of Jerusalem, so I'm asking you to bless Lillian, who is praying for the peace of Jerusalem. Get her out of this house and into Oakcrest as soon as we can."

Not long after, a colleague of mine heard about Lillian's living conditions. This colleague had a friend who was a sales manager at Oakcrest. After hearing Lillian's story, the manager decided to move her to the top of the waiting list.

Within a few weeks, a first-floor unit became available. It only had one bedroom, but it had a den and would be plenty of space for Lillian, even if it didn't meet her three-bedroom preference. We asked Lillian to consider taking the unit, and after thinking about it for a few days, she said she would—but that she wouldn't be happy.

At a follow-up meeting with the sales manager of the community, Lillian disclosed that she wasn't particularly pleased with the unit because

---

61 Psalm 122:6

it didn't have the three bedrooms she requested. This lack, she said, will make her unhappy for the rest of her life.

Hearing an eighty-eight-year-old confess that she's about to make a decision she knows she'll be unhappy with is tough, and the sales manager decided that instead of this unit, she would give Lillian a three-bedroom unit someone had just canceled on that very morning.

By this point, you're probably wondering why Lillian, a lonely widow with no living family, was so fixated on having three bedrooms. As the sole surviving member of her family, she seemed to feel a responsibility to keep all the possessions her sister had upon her death. Lillian knew that without three bedrooms, she'd never fit all those items and her own as well.

Lillian spent two happy years in Oakcrest. While she never unpacked a single box after moving in, she was safe and comfortable.

Sometimes God answers prayers before we even ask.

A few years after my experience with Lillian and her answered prayers, my best friend, Clayton, suddenly passed away. When he died, God already had put in place all the ingredients necessary for his family and me to cope with the loss. I was thankful to be able to call such a great man my best friend, and his family was thankful that God had brought Bev and me into their lives for many purposes. We did not know we had to pray, but God did.

Tools for Financial Planning

In this chapter, we talked about how the dotcom boom made way for the dotcom bust. I also talked about the core values we designed for our company and then introduced you to Lillian and explained how her poverty spirit was holding her back.

After reading this chapter, these are the tools I hope you'll add to your toolbox:

- Understanding the value of an unpopular pick
- Appreciate the gravity of making vows
- Staying out of the poverty mindset

The Value of an Unpopular Pick

Choosing value and dividend stocks for clients during the dotcom boom might not sound exciting, but considering dividends, they were so far out of favor that it made sense. You don't need hedge funds or complicated investment options to make a fair rate of return. Instead, patience and diversification can work wonders. No amount of investment sophistication is going to assure you a significant amount of reward.

Warren Buffett made a bet with hedge funds that a simple S&P 500 Index would beat their portfolios after fees between January 1, 2008, and December 31, 2017.[62] Despite the largest S&P decline since 1974 of 55 percent in 2008 to March 2009, Buffett won, hands down.

Yet, the more money an investor has, the more likely they are to consider alternative investments—and this is fine, as long as those alternatives aren't the bread and butter of a portfolio.

People always hope someone has the secret mojo to help them accumulate vast wealth. There is a temptation to try to find stockbrokers or hedge fund managers who can accelerate your asset accumulation, but the culture of these firms is to accelerate *their* asset accumulation. It's not about being great, comprehensive financial advisors, which is what the public needs today.

The culture of the brokerage firms, insurance companies, and banks selling financial advisory services is to create an illusion that lures the public into a profit trap. It's not that their advisors are bad or even that

---

62 https://www.aei.org/carpe-diem/warren-buffett-wins-1m-bet-made-a-decade-ago-that-the-sp-500-stock-index-would-outperform-hedge-funds/

they do a poor job, it's that an illusion is being sold as a service. Most of the advisors are merely pawns in the company's profit motives.

I wholeheartedly believe that the 2008 downturn happened because financial advisors were not dedicated to the well-being of their clients, simply as a result of the culture of the organizations they're a part of. My firm told our clients well before 2008 that housing prices were ridiculous and that something weird was going on. We repeatedly advised against borrowing excessive amounts to buy a house. If you read books like *The Big Short* that talk about the financial crisis of 2008, they mention the giddiness of Wall Street and the hedge funds that were making so much money at the time.

That's not what people need. They need wealth advisory firms that operate like a medical clinic, holistically analyzing their full situation, from taxes to insurance to investments to estate planning. They need a firm that can serve as a provider of checks and balances to the lawyers, accountants, investment managers, and insurance agents.

Ultimately, financial and physical health are interrelated. If somebody has financial difficulties, it's been proven over time that it will manifest in medical health issues.[63] Financial worries bring stress, and doctors have pointed out the correlation between stress and medical conditions for years.[64]

Making a Vow

Vows are very important and way more powerful than you might realize. Earlier in the book, I talked about how my lunch spending was higher than it needed to be at the start of my career. This was a direct result of

---

63 https://www.purdue.edu/newsroom/purduetoday/releases/2021/Q1/mental-well-being-inherently-connected-to-financial-wellness.html

64 https://www.mayoclinic.org/healthy-lifestyle/stress-management/in-depth/stress-symptoms/art-20050987

child-me vowing, although not consciously, that I wasn't going to eat bad lunches once I was an adult. And it impacted my cash flow for years before I figured it out.

The vows we make, and the blessings or curses offered by others in our lives can have an economic influence for decades. Words spoken within our own hearts or by those with authority over us have a lasting impact, and we need to make sure we learn how to break those curses.

Consider a parent who tells their child they are good for nothing and won't amount to anything in life. Too often, those predictions end up true. Not because the parent had future sight, but because instead of blessing their child, they cursed them. Words spoken over you by people in authority are extremely powerful, and you need to understand what those words were.

The only real way to work around this is to think about the repetitive decisions you make each day. How many of them are the result of a vow you made to yourself, or a negative comment made by a parent or other adult when you were a child? What were your words of blessings or curses and what were your vows? They may be affecting your financial life today and decades later.

Receive the blessings over your life and ask for them to be released, but make a commitment to disavow any curses spoken over your life. You should reject the negative words and ask God to break all curses.

Each of us lives in two worlds at the same time, one physical and one spiritual. The laws of the physical world are exact. If you jump out of an airplane, you fall. If you run into a brick wall, it hurts. These are laws of physics, and they can't be altered or changed.

The forces of the spiritual world operate in a much more judicious way, yet they also work in what *appears* to be an arbitrary way. In other words, you may get mercy and not see a negative impact and the lasting effect. Or, you might get judgment and a negative impact for years. It may seem arbitrary, but there is a perfect judicial system at work.

Someday, when we enter the spiritual world, we will completely understand. I like to say that everyone will live two lives, one in this physical world and one in God's perfect spiritual world. It's there that all that seemed unfair and unjust will be made clear.

What you must remember is that the way you live your life in this physical world will have a significant impact on your next life in the spiritual world. Jesus has all authority in this world and the world to come, which is why knowing Him now is the greatest blessing.

Avoiding the Poverty Spirit

The poverty spirit is a mental or emotional perspective on finance that's completely divorced from your actual financial situation. A person with the poverty spirit has plenty, but always feels that tomorrow, a disaster is coming. They may not be poor, in any way, shape, or form. In fact, they may have quite a bit, but they always believe there's a dark cloud coming, and because of that, they make decisions based on that poverty spirit.

It's a dangerous concept, and none of us are immune to it. I actually find myself having to deal with this in my life, and I have no idea where it came from. It's not easy to get rid of either. Both Beatrice and Lillian, who each had more than $1 million in assets, were living as if in poverty, and even though they could afford better, they both had difficulty accepting that they could.

People with the poverty spirit are consumed with the idea that calamity is imminent. While we used to see this mostly in people born in or around the Great Depression, many thirty- and forty-year-olds, with 2008 very fresh in their memories, also fall victim to this mindset.

Those who live with the poverty spirit believe that there's a dark cloud around every corner and a demon under every rock. They think that they have to protect their job because if they don't, they're going to lose it—possibly as a result of impostor syndrome.

To figure out whether you're suffering the effects of a poverty spirit, look back through your life and consider all the dark clouds and dangers you worried about. Then, think about all the times you remained optimistic about things. If you can't think of any times you were optimistic, and if none of the dangers you've spent your life fearing have come to pass, then you may be afflicted with a poverty spirit.

The truth is, behind every dark cloud is a bright, shining sun. As I mentioned in a prior chapter, two of the world's most successful investors, Charles Schwab and Warren Buffett, are ridiculous optimists. Even in 1987, 2000, and 2008, neither Schwab nor Buffett ever believed that the economic difficulties we faced were anything more than a passing storm—and those were some pretty horrendous periods.

I once read a line that said, "There must be some benefit to worrying, for nothing I ever worried about ever happened." It's true that there's nothing wrong with having a fail-safe or plan B strategy, but the future continues to evolve optimistically, despite setbacks. Remember it is absolutely true that perception is reality. It's as Charles Schwab said in an interview I did in 2020, "Drew, an investor must first and foremost always be an optimist."

Are you?[65]

---

65 For more information about these topics and more, please visit the Financial Consulate's Knowledge Center: https://financialconsulate.com/knowledge-center/

Chapter 7

By 2008 I had really ramped up the company. In addition to myself, I had Chuck Bender and Tim Maurer as advisors and we hired Roger Bair and Sue Fenimore.

I knew the economy was struggling but didn't know we were facing the Great Recession. I began to suspect a problem back in 2006, when a client called me, desperate to have me help his son. The son, a bartender, earning $34,000 per year, had taken a loan on a massive house with mortgage payments totaling $36,000 per year. This situation indicated that lending standards were loosening in a dangerous way and people were buying houses for ridiculous reasons.

Ultimately, the 2008 downturn was logical, and to some degree, you could see it coming because of the excess leverage being used. That's why today's real estate market is nothing compared to that real estate market. In today's market, if you want to buy a house for another 20 percent more than it was worth a year ago, you'd better be ready to put up enough cash and prove beyond a shadow of a doubt you're able to make that mortgage payment.

In 2008, however, nobody cared. They simply made some of the least sensible loans I've ever seen. The real estate agents didn't care, the mortgage brokers didn't care, the appraisers didn't care, the mortgage companies didn't care—and we could not understand why.

Today, it's the exact opposite. Mortgage brokers and mortgage companies are incredibly careful, almost to a fault. Appraisers are independent agents with a professional duty. The lesson to take away from this is that bubbles happen when there's undue leverage. When people pay cash for purchases, you can get overvaluation to some degree, but you're not going to get a bubble pop like we did in 2008. You'll get a bear market, pullback, correction, or rest where markets don't go up for a while and where you'll see less appreciation for a short time, but it's not going to come close to systemic collapse like in 2008.

I always keep in mind something Warren Buffett says: "You only find out who has been swimming naked when the tide goes out."[66] In 2008, thinking about that soon-to-ebb tide, I knew this wasn't going to end pretty, but I didn't know how many naked swimmers we'd end up seeing. I certainly didn't know how bad it was going to get.

Growth Amid Disaster

One of the interesting things about professional advisory firms is that when you go through difficult times, like those we faced in 2008, we tend to grow rapidly during those periods, even though our assets under management might have taken a hit. Our new clients coming in the door tend to go up dramatically, in part because we're so much more proactive and engaged. Clients realize that we are constantly thinking about how a current situation impacts them and should impact their asset allocation, and they want that higher level of service as it seems like the world is crumbling around them.

In 2008 the assets under our management did go down, but not as much as it could have. While this might have felt like a victory, it is not

66 https://money.com/swimming-naked-when-the-tide-goes-out/

worth bragging about. On the negative side, we didn't get fully reinvested as fast as we should have. Clients believe we need to get out before downturns and back in during upturns. I can attest that I may make a good market call, but it may be followed by a bad market call. This is why we try to remain invested over the long run with a well-diversified portfolio.

One good thing that happened in 2008 was that we hired our now CEO Michael McCarthy as an intern. Tim, the advisor who had helped me with Lillian, became an adjunct professor at Towson University where Mike was an accounting student. Just twenty-three years old, Mike was in a tough spot that year. Late to graduate and recently married, he had tried working at an accounting firm as an intern and absolutely hated it.

The experience left him wondering what he could do with an accounting degree when he clearly didn't enjoy accounting. So Mike took the CFP® course Tim was teaching and mentioned his conundrum. Tim suggested he intern with us doing financial planning, putting his accounting background to good use on a wider platform. After joining us, Mike found that working with people and solving their general financial issues was much more fulfilling than simply adding and checking numbers on a spreadsheet.

Ultimately, we remained extremely proactive throughout the downturn and the recovery. We also tried to respond to the particular needs of our clients, some of whom were having a difficult time emotionally dealing with the downturn. One client, who had called us to talk about general market performance rather than the specifics of his portfolio, said he couldn't handle just talking on the phone with us, that he had to see my face. I suggested he come into a meeting, but his request got me thinking. How many clients would prefer to see my face each week as I delivered market updates?

As a result, we decided to do video updates, calling them Financial Pulse, so that clients would be able to see our faces, our eyes, and read our nonverbal communication to better interpret our confidence and understand that it wasn't a smokescreen. These updates were appreciated, and we've kept them going every month since then.[67]

More recently, we have expanded these monthly updates to talk more about general planning, so we're stretching beyond talk of investments, interest rates, and current economic concerns.

Corrections versus Bubbles

At the time this book was written, there was a running gag about the difficulty people were having buying houses. In some markets, real estate was moving so quickly, people joked about having to buy properties before they looked at them, making offers that far exceeded the asking price.

For those who lived through the housing bubble and Great Recession of 2008, this situation is making people understandably nervous. To the uninitiated, it might seem like an indication of another housing bubble, especially when it's combined with the excessive inflation and rocky stock market.

I'm not convinced people should be worried, however. Markets will always go up and down. These are normal corrections—nothing stays flat. The problems occur when we have excess leverage, which we definitely did in 2008.

Consider the crash of 1929. In 1929, buying stocks on margin—in other words, borrowing a brokerage firm's money to put additional holdings in your portfolio—was not as tightly regulated.[68] This led to millions of dollars moving from banks to brokerage houses to facilitate stock purchases for investors with very little money. The thought process behind this loose lending was that brokerage firms could always sell the

---

67 https://financialconsulate.com/knowledge-center/financial-pulse/
68 https://www.finra.org/rules-guidance/key-topics/margin-accounts

stock to repay the margin debt. Once the stock market began to slip and stocks lost value, this created a catastrophe.

Likewise, lending standards for real estate in the early 2000s were notoriously low. Liar's loans, which required no documentation to verify a borrower's stated income, were very common. In a similar vein to what happened in the 1920s, the prevailing theory in the early 2000s was, if a person can't afford their home, the lender can foreclose and sell it.

This idea was supported by real estate statistics that hadn't shown a widespread downturn in real estate prices for decades. This made a lot of sense at the time, especially since you could put a house on the market in the early 2000s and sell it for as much as 50 percent more than you paid for it six months to two years prior.

Between the embedded belief that real estate would not go down in value and that Fed chair Alan Greenspan was some kind of wizard who would figure out how to hold the economy up, even if real estate prices went down, absolute foolish lending occurred.

Today, lending standards are much more stringent. The rise in real estate prices is not being driven by excess leverage, it is being driven by a supply shortage. This shortage is a result of ten years of underinvestment in real estate during and after the Great Recession.

Avoiding Excess Personal Leverage

The banks and other financial institutions did a poor job in the early 2000s by lending too many people too much money that they could never hope to pay back. While the banks do have a responsibility (in the very least, to their shareholders) to lend more responsibly, consumers also have to understand their limits and repayment capabilities.

Understanding both limits and repayment possibilities requires consumers to be direct and honest with themselves. Consider student loans, an area some say is in crisis right now. Often, there is no economic connection between the potential salary a student can expect to earn after graduation and the amount of money they borrow and the interest rate they have to pay on their loan. The same thing was true in the real estate market in the early 2000s. The mortgage companies didn't care how much they were lending and who they were lending to, but a lender's willingness to give someone money should not dictate a borrower's acceptance.

Instead, looking at the hard numbers—the amount of the loan, the income of the borrower, the cash flow—that should all drive a borrower's decision to take the money. Because student loans are guaranteed by the federal government, banks and universities take advantage of students' naivete to loan them ridiculous sums for a potential career that cannot pay back the debt. College tuition is a classic bubble created by foolish government guarantees.

Tools for Financial Planning

Talking about 2008 and the Great Recession is always difficult, but there are some fantastic lessons we can take away from that experience. These lessons, when applied to our own financial lives, can help insulate us from the next bubble so we fare far better than our contemporaries. The tools I want to give you after reading this chapter include:

- The importance of introspection
- Wisely used debt
- The irrational market

The Importance of Introspection

Introspection is the ability of an individual to examine and analyze their own actions and thoughts, ultimately leading to self-improvement through accountability. Regardless of how powerful introspection can be, many people instead focus on *outrospection*. This is the process of blaming everything on someone, or something outside of yourself.

The majority of people, when things go wrong in their life, blame others—their children, their spouse, their boss, their parents, and so on. If you can flip that switch from looking outward to looking inward, it is the greatest asset you will ever have in your entire life.

Blaming others does not solve anything. Maybe it gives you an excuse so you feel like you can avoid guilt or anger toward yourself, but it will never help you fix the situation you're in. Instead, when you can admit that you are responsible for what's happening—that you made the error or exercised poor judgment—then you can think about what actions you can take to change the outcome.

When my wife and I were struggling with different ideas of spending limitations, I could very easily have just blamed her since the only problem I initially saw was credit card usage, and it was her signature on those purchases. Instead, I used the power of introspection to look at my own actions and thought processes. That's what helped me realize that I was probably more to blame than she was.

I clearly communicated to her, "I love money more than I love you." As I intentionally changed my message to "I love you unconditionally," she responded with her own change. As I changed my mindset toward money and my communications with Bev, she began to think differently toward me, and the miraculous change between us took place.

So many people go to work each day feeling dread because their bosses are legitimately terrible. But if they only focus on that—if they only outrospect—then they may not realize they need to build their skills and expand their networks so they can get a different job with a better boss. In some cases, it may be that the boss you think is terrible is actually trying to drive you to be better, and with introspection, you might realize that and see the changes you need to make to better that relationship. Maybe your boss bears some incredible personal pressures you do not know about. Maybe you need to develop the skills to deal with difficult people for a greater calling in the future.

It has been proven time and time again that people who overspend tend not to overspend because they're just poor at economics but because of things going on in their personal lives that they're not willing to address.[69] Whether you're spending out of insecurity, boredom, loneliness, or habit after growing up watching your family do the same, introspection can give you the insight to figure that out and change the situation.

Refusing to be introspective about spending isn't just potentially holding you back economically, it could be bringing on financial disaster. We had clients around 2007, a married couple from New York, who owned a beautiful property in West Palm Beach. In prior years, their net worth had been as high as $80 million, but due to their poor spending habits, their only remaining assets were a portfolio of about $2 million and their Florida home, which was worth about $4 million.

It was difficult to believe this couple could have gone from $80 million to just $6 million in net worth, but after visiting their New York apartment, full of gorgeous artwork and antique furniture, I immediately saw the vestiges of their spent wealth.

Tim and I looked over the couple's finances and realized that their situation was virtually hopeless unless they sold the house in Florida. If they didn't, they would likely go bankrupt. This was in 2007, and while the housing market hadn't collapsed, it was teetering. They had already dropped the price of their Florida property, but they weren't getting any interest from buyers. On one of the art-covered walls of their apartment, I saw an embroidered scripture from decades ago that one of their relatives

---

69 https://resources.depaul.edu/financial-fitness/tackle-overspending/Pages/reasons-we-overspend.aspx

had made. I pointed to the scripture and told them that at this point, reducing the price wasn't going to help, but God might.

I prayed with them in that apartment, and a week later, somebody offered them about $4 million for the house. They managed to sell the place in the nick of time. We invested the proceeds for them, and within eight months of the miraculous situation that saved them from total ruin, they were ripping money out of that account, easily spending $600,000 a year out of a $6 million account.

You don't need a calculator or a securities license to tell you that $6 million isn't going to last long when you're spending $600,000 a year. We chose to disengage with this client.

We then took a look at their spending and one of the simplest and most striking expenses they had—and needed to cut—was their penchant for each having two Starbucks drinks per day. Totaling about $175 per week, that Starbucks habit could easily cost them $1 million over twenty years, when you consider interest that could've been earned on that money.

Spending that kind of money at Starbucks is fine if you can truly afford it, but few people can. Yet when an expense like this is broken down into small daily increments, it seems so insignificant. That's why it's important to take time for introspection to explore your spending habits and determine whether you need to change them.

Wisely Used Debt

Debt is understandably confusing because, when used wisely, it can be your best friend, yet it is also public enemy number one. The human psyche wants to be debt-free. Even people who think they're risk takers technically want to be debt-free. Often, when you meet people who are heavily in debt, they tend to be very high strung. Part of the reason, in my opinion, is that the human psyche doesn't like wheeling and dealing in so much debt.

This is all great information to heed so you don't become overly indebted, but we can't ignore the fact that debt used wisely can be your best friend. For example, if you buy a house with a reasonable amount of leverage, and that house appreciates in value, then that leverage is going to make you more money than many of your other financial moves. But borrowing hundreds of thousands of dollars to send your kid to college or to buy a house in a poor location could financially devastate you.

The first key to keeping debt on your good side is to understand *why* you're borrowing money and why the interest cost will be beneficial—which means comparing the cost of the debt against the potential of the investment.

For example, let's say you're thinking of buying a house. You have to live somewhere, and if you decided to rent, it would cost you at least $2,000 a month. If you can buy and spend just $2,500 a month, that means you're only spending an extra $500 for a place you will eventually own. In addition, you could potentially get some tax deductions on that extra cost. Of course, those savings are offset by your maintenance costs on the home. But if it's appreciating enough in value, that will more than offset the maintenance costs.

This is why agents always say that when it comes to real estate, it's about location, location, location. First, you think about location, and after you finish thinking of location, you think of location, and after you think of a location, you think of location again. Is someone going to want that house from you in the future because of where it's located? Why did California real estate become so popular and so expensive? Because of the location—its weather, climate, proximity to Silicon Valley, and so forth. It was a great location.

Why do you buy the house in the best public school district possible? Because parents are going to try to relocate to a place where their kids can get the best education without it costing them a nickel more. If all education had to be paid for, parents would live anywhere they felt and find a school for their kid, but they go to those school districts because it's a great school district, it's free, and all they have to do is own a house in that area.

Part of the reason I moved to Florida was not just the taxes and the weather, but also because I strongly believe that as long as Florida doesn't change the way it runs its cities and taxes its citizens, people are going to flock here. They will come because the weather's better, the taxation is better, and because of technology, you can live and work anywhere you choose.

One thing to keep in mind, as I think too many people make this mistake—don't buy a home and borrow money just for the tax deductions. To pay $1 to a bank to save $0.30 on your tax return is silly. The key to intelligent borrowing is to consider the opportunity cost of what you're borrowing and what you think you're going to make on that money.

This is the same equation that students should use when they are encouraged to borrow money for college. If you borrow that amount at that interest rate, what is it going to do economically for you? Can you justify that equation with enough safety based on your future earnings?

Debt used wisely is your best friend, but the human psyche wants to always be debt-free, so be careful about how you use debt, even if the debt offers you a good opportunity for gains. If you make a mistake or something goes wrong, you still have to repay that debt.

The Irrational Market

A lot of people think they can time the market or predict its direction. They won't use those words exactly, but you'll hear them say things like, "I'm going to sell because the market's going to go down because it's overvalued." Or, "I'm going to wait for [event] to sell," or "I'm not going to sell this speculative position because I think it will come back sooner or later."

The problem with these lines of thought, and others like them, is that markets are irrational and can continue to be irrational far longer than you can be solvent. Economist John Maynard Keynes first said that in the 1930s.[70] Focused primarily on stocks and bonds, Keynes made investments on leverage. While he generally felt confident about the long-term prospects of his investments, he ultimately had to have a point where he would sell. Why? Because he knew that the market wasn't sensible, it was irrational—and it could be so much longer than he could afford.

When investor Jean-Marie Eveillard created a gold fund in 1993, gold had been in a thirteen-year bear market, and he thought that was about to change.[71] He was right, but it wasn't until about 1999 that it finally changed. It took six years from when he created that gold fund to when it started panning out. Thankfully, he remained solvent through that time. But there may have come a time when he had to give up—and I'm betting he knew what that point was.

Every investor needs to understand at what point they have to give up when a market or investment isn't fulfilling their "hunch." If the market's going down, don't assume that it's going up anytime soon, even if you think that valuations are cheap. If markets start going up, don't assume they're going to stop going up because you're smarter than the market

70 https://www.nasdaq.com/articles/the-markets-can-remain-irrational-longer-than-you-can-remain-solvent-2020-07-01

71 https://www.fa-mag.com/news/jean-marie-eveillard-protege-dies-at-37-16011.html

and there's too much bad news for the market to go much higher. Also, don't be too confident that once that momentum heads in one direction or the other, it takes a lot for it to stop. The market is its own beast. You can't predict what it will do—even if you constantly study charts and historic performance.

If you're betting against the market going higher, you'd better think twice. And if you're holding on because you believe that the market can't go any lower, don't count on it. Markets can be far more irrational than you can be logical. Just make sure you can sit it out if you're going to.

Now, when I say "sit it out," I'm not talking about being able to sit out your uncomfortable emotions. You should never make a decision to get out because of your emotions. You should make decisions to move because there's an economic danger to you to stay put the way you're invested. So, if you can't *financially* sit it out, get out.

A great example of the irrationality of the market is found in the Dutch tulip mania of the 1600s. At that time, the price of tulips began to climb right along with the flower's popularity. By 1636, investors began buying what essentially amounted to futures contracts to secure bulbs at the end of the season, thereby speculating over the flower's rise in value—and betting a lot of money on this eventuality.[72]

Almost overnight, people went from paying a few cents for a tulip bulb to suddenly paying a few dollars. The next thing you know, they're paying a year's wages to buy tulip bulbs. This lasted for about three months, at which time the supply of tulip bulbs became so enormous that the price crumbled.[73]

Never again have tulip bulbs sold for anything even remotely close to those prices, not in the 400 years since. While tulip mania ravaged the finances of many Dutch families, we reap the benefit today when you

---

72 https://mises.org/library/dutch-monetary-environment-during-tulipmania
73 https://en.wikipedia.org/wiki/File:Tulip_price_index1.svg

visit the Netherlands and see enormous fields covered with the beautiful flowers. But don't just be dazzled by their beauty—think of them as a reminder of how unpredictable the market can be and how important it is to have a plan to maintain your solvency amid the market's irrationality.[74]

---

74 For more information about these topics and more, please visit the Financial Consulate's Knowledge Center: https://financialconsulate.com/knowledge-center/

Chapter 8

The Financial Consulate emerged from the 2008 downturn with some new clients and a new chief operating and compliance officer (CCO), Mike McCarthy, in 2010. No longer an intern, Mike had grown right along with our business and was proving himself an invaluable asset. When you find a buried treasure, you bring it out for your enrichment. Mike McCarthy was a buried treasure, and fortunately, we saw his amazing potential and brought him forth for the enrichment of the clients, employees, and company.

As financial advisors, we spend a lot of time educating clients. One of the biggest areas we need to educate them in is proper estate planning. One problem folks face when estate planning is figuring out what advisor-given advice is bad.

We had one client, Susan, come to us after she received $400,000 from her deceased husband's insurance policies. The first thing she wanted to do was pay off her house, and the advisor she had been working with vehemently told her that was a horrible idea and not to do it. Boy, was that some bad advice.

Getting Debt-Free and Canceling an Annuity

As you read in the last chapter, I believe that humans want to be debt-free. Too often, advisors counsel clients to maintain a low-interest debt and invest the funds they would otherwise use to pay off that debt, because you can earn more on the investment than you spend on the debt. But this is pure fabrication created by the economic bias of financial advisors.

Let's think about this objectively. If you do not pay off your mortgage and instead put a lump sum in the market and the market goes down, let's say 30, 40, or 50 percent, the mortgage company doesn't call you up and discount your mortgage by the amount you lost. We don't know what the future holds for the market, and again, as mentioned in the last chapter, the market can remain irrational longer than any of us may remain solvent.

I do believe that the market will continue to go higher, but I don't know the overall route it will take to get there. Further, I believe in the power of being debt-free for people. When you're in debt, your psyche often feels a sense of enslavement to that debt. While there are people who can be in debt and still keep a relatively healthy attitude about their debt, it's rare. The average human being wants to be debt-free, because debt is like a ball and chain tied around you.

So when we determine whether a client should pay off their home with a lump sum, we analyze it by considering:

- What are we giving up if we pay it off?
- What's the mortgage?
- What's the interest rate?
- What's the client's psyche?
- How are they investing their money?

Thankfully, Susan ignored her advisor's advice on paying off the house and she ultimately did it, praise God. Then the advisor convinced her to buy an annuity and a municipal bond fund. He told her that the municipal bond fund was like liquid money, and the annuity was the "sure money." This isn't necessarily untrue, but the particular annuity he sold her had a fifteen-year deferred sales charge on it. And the advisor's commission on this sale? It was around 15 percent.

This was all the money Susan had in the world. She needed it to live on. She had a little pension, received some Social Security, and had a part-time job, but it wasn't enough to sustain her, so she would definitely need to dip into the annuity and bond fund—which meant she'd definitely be paying penalties.

She'd heard about us and came to visit one day. She told us her situation and asked, "Do you think what's been going on here is right?"

I said, "No."

She wanted our help to fix the situation, so I brought in the Maryland State Securities Commissioner. The commissioner saw that the agent had gone beyond his purview as an insurance agent and had given what essentially amounted to financial planning advice, and the commissioner gave him a choice: figure out how to reverse the annuity sale, or face action for doing financial planning without being a financial planner.

Ultimately, he got the company to reverse the annuity and give Susan her money back—and just in time because the downturn happened soon after.

The agent also unwound her from the municipal bond fund. While these funds can be a great fit for some clients, this tax-free fund was unnecessary for a woman making $35,000 a year who was barely in the 10 percent tax bracket.

Sadly, we see this type of thing all the time; people come to us with ridiculous amounts of money in high-commission investments where the advisors routinely do nothing and take high commissions and fees. High commission can lock you into an investment for a long time.

Any investment made should allow you to sell and invest in a different direction at any time, without penalty. Annuities can now be bought commission-free, so be careful buying one with surrender charges.

Consolidation in Estate Planning

While it's easy to make mistakes after inheriting assets, it's also easy to make mistakes when you're planning your estate.

I remember Mary who, around 2002, came to us just after her mother had died, leaving behind certificates from 110 different bonds and stock companies. Because her mom had had multiple positions in each company as well as multiple bonds from each issuer, Mary inherited roughly 750 different certificates and bond registrations, all of which were stuffed in safe deposit boxes or in folders around the house. None of her mom's holdings were registered with brokerage firms, which meant Mary had to send a death certificate, a letter of testamentary, and an affidavit of domicile to each and every company.

Can you imagine the amount of work that was? And time? If her mother had known, she might have instead consolidated her holdings in one brokerage firm so Mary would have had a much easier time transferring assets after death—and so there were no assets left unclaimed.

Some people believe that having multiple portfolios with a variety of broker-dealers is a good idea, but in today's world, there's no reason to have diversified holdings throughout different brokerage firms. Securities are not handled today the way they were during the Great Depression. At that time, if a brokerage firm went under, your securities went with it.

Today, even when a brokerage firm goes under, it's difficult to actually lose your holdings since it's all digital, and there is a central depository where certificates are accounted for. If somebody at Schwab's sells AT&T and somebody at Merrill Lynch buys AT&T, the central depository just says, "Merrill now has this many shares of AT&T, and Schwab has this many." In the old days, they would actually move certificates from one brokerage firm to another, but they no longer need to do that.

In recent years, you may have heard of a brokerage firm called Robinhood restricting trading on certain stocks.[75] This could make you understandably uneasy about having all your holdings with one brokerage, but if you understand what was going on behind the scenes at Robinhood, you'd see why this was a rare issue.

At the time trading was restricted, Robinhood clients were overly focused on buying volatile stocks on margin—introducing a lot of uncertainty about whether they would be able to fulfill a margin call when their share values plummeted.

When a brokerage's clientele is primarily made up of margin buyers and speculative investors, it can result in special measures, such as restricted trading.

Another type of brokerage to avoid consolidating with is one that has too many short sales on the books. Short selling is a process that involves the brokerage essentially "lending" shares of a stock to a client who wants to make a bet on a position falling in value. The client, who sells the borrowed shares to other investors, must rebuy the position and return the borrowed shares by a certain date. The hope is that by the time they have to rebuy, the shares will be far less expensive than they were when they were borrowed and sold.

Regardless, should a brokerage fail, investors can look to the Securities Investor Protection Corporation (SIPC) for $500,000 in protection.[76] Many brokerages go even further, relying on Lloyd's of London for supplemental protection for clients.

It's also helpful to look at history. When Lehman Brothers collapsed in 2008, clients who held any stock or bond that was not Lehman stock

75 https://www.cnbc.com/2021/01/28/robinhood-interactive-brokers-restrict-trading-in-gamestop-s.html

76 https://www.sipc.org

or Lehman bonds simply had them transferred to their new brokerage firm. This happens much like a bank after being taken over by the FDIC.

While the brokerage firm behind your portfolio likely won't spell disaster, your choice of financial advisory firm can. In addition to the many points made in this book about finding a skilled, educated, credentialed, and experienced advisor who approaches planning like a doctor of personal finance, you also want to focus on a firm with multiple advisors. It's never a good idea to put your million dollars of investments and your financial well-being into the hands of a one-person shop who could easily get sick, retire, or even pass away unexpectedly. It's not that easy to get your assets to another advisor who truly understands your goals, objectives, and risk profile. Somebody who doesn't work with you day in, day out, can't just walk in the door and take over your accounts and have it be an effective switch.

As so often happens, there were enough issues with Mary's situation that even consolidation wouldn't have helped. You can probably imagine, with 750 certificates lying around, Mary's mother's big passion was investing. She loved evaluating investments and buying them, and Mary knew that. This gave the certificates a nostalgic appeal, much as a handcrafted quilt might have.

Because Mary had that emotional attachment to these certificates, when her mom died in 2000, she could not let them go. So instead of evaluating the investments and considering what should be sold, she held everything. Sadly, her mom had a lot of tech and communications stocks that ended up going down dramatically during that 2001-2002 downturn. It took almost four years before Mary finally gave us permission to truly manage the holdings.

Mary's situation, with holdings scattered in various places, was not as unique as you might think. Around 2014, a new client named Chip came to see us. His mother had passed away two years earlier, and the estate was nowhere near being resolved. Chip's mother had held as many as sixty different securities with a variety of transfer agents in stock certificate form. Chip had a lawyer helping him, but the lawyer would only give him general information about what he needed to do and made no suggestions for streamlining the situation.

When Chip came to us, we basically took him by the hand and started accumulating all those assets into a single estate account. Then, we worked with the lawyer to finalize the estate administration. It took us more than a year to get that done—and even when we thought it was completed, it wasn't. Because every year for the six years that followed, we would receive a letter about another security that needed to get transferred over to Chip.

The big takeaway here is that you're not doing anyone any favors by holding assets in a variety of places. In today's world, they should all be accumulated into one brokerage firm. Rarely should a security be held in certificate form in a safe deposit box or at home. Stock certificates should be deposited in a discount broker like Schwab, Vanguard, or Fidelity. You should have one or at most two banks. Only your checking account should be joint with a responsible child/children.

Tools for Financial Planning

In this chapter, I shared many examples of estate planning gone wrong. While we often see the result of those mistakes after a person's death, they are easily avoided well before death if you just pay attention to these three financial planning concepts:

- Economic bias
- Risk management
- Diversification versus concentration

Exploring Your Advisor's Economic Bias

When a financial planner offers you products or services, they do so with their own economic bias. Understanding your advisor's bias gives you a better ability to deal with that person and make sure that you get what's best for you, rather than what suits that individual's wallet.

Think about it this way—if you go into a restaurant, you know immediately that the person waiting on your table has an economic bias that the more you buy and the more you drink, the larger your tab will be and the higher the tip should be. You don't look at them negatively because they have an economic bias, but you understand that it's there, and that makes you a better consumer.

You cannot eliminate all economic biases. Everyone has an economic bias, no matter what. Some economic biases are not easy to understand. For example, property and casualty insurance agents have an economic bias to undersell auto and home insurance because their compensation is increased if they undersell (I'll explain this in more detail later in the chapter). A lawyer's economic bias is time. They can't spend all the time in the world to develop the best will and estate documents for you, since you probably won't be willing to pay for the time that would take. Therefore, their economic bias is to get you to make decisions as quickly as possible, yet it's not necessarily always prudent to make such important decisions in haste.

Understanding economic biases of the people you're dealing with can make you a much better consumer. When the service or product provider *tells* you their economic bias, it shows a level of integrity that can help you decide whether to do business with them. Earlier in this chapter, I told you about Susan, who had inherited a $400,000 life insurance death benefit after her husband died. She'd immediately wanted to pay off her house, but her advisor said she shouldn't. He didn't tell her that he didn't want her to because his economic bias was to have her leave as much money under his management as possible. A fee-only advisor with a fiduciary responsibility, however, must tell her whether they have an economic bias and then demonstrate how their advice wasn't influenced by that bias.

At the Financial Consulate, it's a principle of our firm that economic biases should be stated. For example, if we have a client who wants to pay off their mortgage, we will explain that we have an economic bias against them doing that, since it means we won't have that money to invest any longer. When we state that, we are in no way suggesting the client not pay off their mortgage; we are simply disclosing that our economic bias is to have them hold those funds and invest them, but that we are not going to allow that bias to impact the guidance we give them.

From there, we begin the process of looking at the interest rate on the mortgage, the client's attitude toward debt, their risk profile, the risk and return potential after tax of saved and invested funds, and so on.

Ideally, everyone should work with an advisor who puts their economic bias on the table so they can see that the advisor is trying to be transparent and the client can make the best decision for themselves—not the best decision for their advisor.

Being a fee-only advisor lessens the economic biases I have, but this doesn't mean I was a bad person before I was fee-only. I was a good person in 1995 before I went fee-only, but because I had the economic biases of the commissions paid on insurance and investments, it affected the way I helped my clients with their planning. I became a dramatically better financial advisor when I got away from that.

Now, my job is to educate and supervise what my clients are doing, making sure that they get what's best for them, whereas before, my focus was more on selling them a product. You want your doctor to be as bias-free as they can be, suggesting the best medical advice for you, regardless of their own compensation.

Only independent, fee-only advisors who are fiduciaries are obligated to work with you as free of bias as possible.

Risk Management or Insurance Sales?

Risk management is the process of analyzing perils and determining how to best mitigate them. One of the possible mitigation methods is with insurance. I generally ask four questions when assessing a client's risks:

1. If this risk occurs, what economic damage will happen to the client, their beneficiaries, or their loved ones? The key is to insure the most devastating risks.

2. What is the statistical likelihood that this will happen? The key is to insure the most likely risks.

3. What are some ways to mitigate the damage if it happens? The key is looking for low-cost ways to minimize the impact.

4. What amount of money can we budget toward mitigating the damage and provide financial resources if necessary? The key is you cannot insure every risk, so your insurance budget has to be allocated efficiently.

It's a very logical process that all companies use in their businesses and every individual should use as well. When you ask yourself these questions, you can see that certain risk-mitigating products, like long-term care insurance, are extremely valuable because they cover expensive risks with a high statistical likelihood. Yet others, like cancer insurance, are illogical from a risk management perspective—because rather than getting covered for only one illness, you can get medical insurance, life insurance, and disability insurance to give you a broader spectrum of coverage from a variety of illnesses.

When we consider life insurance for our clients, we look at it from a risk management perspective. We want to make sure that the surviving spouse and children are protected, but then we need to consider to what extent we want to protect them. That will depend on whether the other spouse is working, and, if they are, how likely they are to keep their job after their spouse passes away. We also need to think about what kind of help they will need in the household, what kind of debt they have, and what their college funding plans are for the kids.

Then, we take it into the future and think about what happens when those children are twenty-one or twenty-two and they graduate from college. What is the client's financial position likely to be then? Is there a strong likelihood they will have paid off their house? Will they have been saving and accumulating for retirement? How will their risks have changed at that point?

I would easily say that about 90 percent of the people who come to us have very poorly designed insurance policies.

Often, cash value-accumulating, whole life insurance policies appeal to a client's greed side. They are shown this potential cash value accumulation and, compared to the premiums paid in, it seems attractive. But that doesn't make the policy a good fit from a risk management perspective.

Cash value policies are very important for certain types of risk, such as managing certain estate tax issues or planning for a special needs child. Too often, however, these policies are sold simply because the commissions are higher than term policies.

Life insurance isn't the only area with problems. When you go to buy personal auto insurance and homeowners' insurance, the agent you work with is not a risk manager. They're not thinking about it from a risk management perspective. Instead, they may give you enough coverage to satisfy the law or a lender, while ensuring that they get a bonus for fewer claims.

Law versus Risk

Auto insurance is a legally required coverage. But there is a big difference between buying insurance to satisfy your legal responsibilities and buying insurance to manage your risk. The purpose of insurance is to prevent your personal economic disaster.

When you put an auto policy together, you want to do a risk management analysis, and that begins with analyzing the power of deductibles. First, you want to know how the premium is affected by raising and lowering your deductibles. Then you want to choose a deductible that has a high enough effect on your premium to make it worthwhile, and determine whether you can afford to pay it. So, if you hit a deer and your car's got $3,500 of damage, can you afford to pay the first $500 or $1,000, which is the deductible? If you do that, will it offer you significant enough savings each year over a smaller deductible? And if you do that instead of a zero deductible or $200 deductible, will you save enough money to make it worthwhile?

The other angle to consider is that you want to make only large claims with the insurance company, not small ones, because just two claims in a year can cause all kinds of increases in premiums on your policy, even if they're just small claims. I know this in part because it happened to me.

In 2004 I hit a car parked behind me and submitted a claim, my first ever in the history of my policy. About a year later, I got a pamphlet in the mail from the insurance company saying they would fix any dings in my windshield for free. I called the agent, and he explained they like to fix those kinds of problems early so the windshield doesn't weaken and break entirely. I decided to take advantage of the offer and get the windshield fixed.

A month and a half later, I got a fifteen 15 percent increase in premium. It turns out that the windshield fix was considered a second claim.

Next with auto insurance, you have to ask yourself whether you should just go with the minimum state insurance requirements or secure more coverage. We generally advise clients to get at least $500,000/person $1,000,000/accident, and $100,000 for property damage in liability coverage. In addition, we want the same amounts for uninsured motorist coverage, which has a variety of state requirements. Over 12 percent of drivers on the road are uninsured, and 50 percent drive with state minimum coverage, leaving you overly exposed to risk if you are in an accident involving an uninsured or underinsured driver.[77]

Earlier, I talked about the economic bias your advisor might have. When it comes to auto and home insurance, the agent's economic bias is to keep the auto insurance to the most reasonable level possible, because they get a lot of money in a bonus if they don't have a lot of big claims against the premiums they bring in. If you weren't aware of this, here's how it works:

Let's say you buy a policy with $100,000 / $300,000 of personal injury liability coverage. That means if you have an accident and there's one person hurt, you'll give them up to $100,000. The second number, $300,000, means that if there are three people in the accident, you'll give no more than $300,000 to all the people in the accident, and no one person gets more than $100,000.

Then there's a third number, which stands for the property damage limit. So if you hit a family's car and they're driving a Porsche SUV, it might be $75,000 in property damage, but the most they can receive is that third number.

Insurance companies look at the car you drive, where you live, and your driving record, and that's what your premium is based on. At the end of the year, your agent has a total amount of premium collected from you and all their other clients. The insurance company looks at the

---

77 https://www.iii.org/fact-statistic/facts-statistics-uninsured-motorists

difference between what the agent collected in premiums and what the company had to pay out in claims to those clients. They then award the agent with a bonus based on the difference.

So, if your agent collects $2 million in premiums but the company only pays out $1.2 million for claims of your agent's clients, then he may get a bonus paid on the $800,000 of profitable premiums difference.

When you work with a fee-based advisor, like those at the Financial Consulate, there is no economic bias driven by these bonuses. We may suggest a client purchase an umbrella liability policy with $1 million or more coverage, depending on the client's net worth. The umbrella policy will umbrella both your car and home if a claim is made for greater than the underlying auto and home policy liability coverage. It may cost as little as $150 per year to get $1 million in umbrella coverage—that's how affordable it is.

Because of the lower premium (which offers a very low commission) and the higher limit on potential claim payouts, these higher-coverage policies can wreak havoc with an agent's potential bonus, which, in my opinion, is why they rarely suggest them to clients. Remember, the purpose of insurance is not to pay for small amounts of claims but instead to prevent personal economic disaster.

Getting a Go-Between

I believe that an advisor who wants to model themselves like a doctor of personal finance should always be the go-between for you and an insurance agent or investment broker, much like a medical doctor is your go-between with the medical and pharmaceutical companies.

Imagine if a pharmaceutical company could call you on the phone and say, "Do you have psoriasis? Well, I have a pill for $50 a month that will solve that for one year. You take it, and at the end of the year, you'll never have psoriasis again." Imagine being able to call Pfizer and say,

"You know, I'm feeling a little heart valve blockage. Do you happen to have anything that could help me relieve that?" And they send you statin drugs because you feel like you have a heart problem.

This would be a nightmare scenario, and yet it's exactly what the public does when calling an insurance company or agent and dealing with them directly. Every day we see brilliant people—lawyers, accountants, entrepreneurs—really smart folks, and the minute we review their insurance coverage, we see that they have absolutely the wrong coverage for their needs and their risks.

Nobody should sit down with an insurance agent without first consulting an advisor who acts like a doctor of personal finance and *then* bring the insurance agent in. Put that advisor between you and the insurance industry so you can ensure that you're really considering the risks and benefits of each approach.

No matter what, whenever you buy insurance, you must make sure it's about risk management. Risk management is looking at:

- What risk are you worried about?
- How can you mitigate the risk, if at all?
- What resources do you have to help handle the risk if it occurs?
- Can/should you insure the risk with a third-party like an insurance company?

Risk management is logical, economic driven, and unemotional. Agents are not trained in risk management. Further, as they develop a book of business with thousands of clients, they don't have time to look through client files and contact them to update insurance as their life situations change.

Bonus: Beneficiaries

Because we talked so much about estate planning in this chapter, I thought it was important to add a bonus financial planning tool dealing with beneficiary elections. Most people think that if they go to a lawyer and write a will, they've done their estate planning, but nothing could be further from the truth.

When it comes to your portfolio, bank accounts, retirement accounts, and insurance policies, titling and beneficiaries trump your will. In other words, if you intend to leave the contents of your personal bank account to your children but it's titled as a joint account with your new spouse, the children will not be able to take the money. If you want to leave your IRA account to a new spouse, but your sibling is still listed with the IRA custodian as the beneficiary, then your sibling will get the funds.

If your beneficiaries are incorrect, then your assets will go to the wrong people. Period. End of story. The Supreme Court has made that ruling. Most lawyers, when they write your will, will notify you about your beneficiaries, but that leaves you with the job of figuring out what accounts need to be updated. Worse, it's only a single reminder.

At the Financial Consulate, the goal is to review the beneficiaries on all the investment accounts we hold for a client every time we meet with them, which is normally at least once or twice a year. Believe it or not, over 25 percent of the time, we change something on those beneficiary designations.

The biggest mistake people make is oversimplifying the beneficiary designation. Let's say you want to leave your life insurance death benefit to your spouse and then equally to your two children. Your primary beneficiary is your spouse and your children, Austin and Melanie, are your contingent beneficiaries with a fifty-fifty split.

When you write it like this, if your spouse and Austin predecease you, Melanie would get 100 percent of the inheritance from that retirement account, and your grandchildren through Austin would get nothing.

You need to work with an advisor who can help you word that designation properly so that Austin's family receives some of that benefit in the event of his death.

Diversification versus Concentration

Many of the stories I shared in this chapter involved people who had diversified their assets. Both Mary's and Chip's mothers had assets spread over many sectors, different investment types, and unfortunately, different locations.

While diversification is definitely a critical component to managing risk, it's important to remember that concentration can also be a great strategy for those who want to grow their wealth. In fact, I will be the first to tell you, here and now, that my richest clients have always gotten that way because of concentration, not because of diversification.

Fundamentals matter, especially when it comes to concentration. When a client has a high concentration in a blue chip company that has been around for a long time and has done exceptionally well for the last twenty or thirty years, it can make that client millions just to remain invested. It's not just old companies that help clients get rich with concentration. My wealthiest client, worth close to $50 million, has made his money off a start-up biotech company.

Yes, people with highly concentrated investments do need to consider diversification to remain wealthy, but that doesn't mean they should sell all or most of their concentrated position. They might need to sell a small portion, or we might need to diversify their other assets. We can also put a plan in place to lock in gains if the stock starts to fall.

Concentration can build wealth, and diversification can preserve it, but that doesn't necessarily mean you have to diversify yourself out of every concentrated position. You have to determine what level of concentration you're willing to have in a specific company. You need to make sure you understand the company relatively well, including having an idea of how certain events might affect the stock. For example, what would happen if the company's founder or CEO died? You also want to make sure the company has a reasonable upward trajectory.

Financial advisors who heavily push diversification and rebalancing have an economic bias to advise these moves, as they make fees or commissions on the purchase and sale of investments. Does that mean they are wrong every time? Not at all. But it is important to understand what they will gain if you sell and diversify.[78] How much in taxes must be paid? What about an exchange fund? What about a charitable trust?

There are many solutions, but advisors seem to be focused on selling and reinvesting with them.

---

78 For more information about these topics and more, please visit the Financial Consulate's Knowledge Center: https://financialconsulate.com/knowledge-center/

Chapter 9

By the time the Financial Consulate entered 2014, we had figured out a lot of company dynamics. We'd survived myriad staffing problems and had a group of young financial professionals who were excited and dedicated to our clients' success. Chris and I had listened to God's message and reworked the radio show to reflect that message.

Expanding Tax Services

Business was rolling along nicely in 2014, but not everything we attempted went exactly as planned. During that year, we decided to buy a tax practice in Gettysburg that had quite a few clients. Initially, our goal was to maintain those tax clients and bring them over to the financial planning side, while also using the tax planning resources for our existing financial planning clients.

Sadly, most of the tax clients had brokers with firms like Ameriprise, Edward Jones, and Morgan Stanley and didn't see the need to leave these commissioned advisors. To this day, many of these clients are still dealing with financial planning departments that are not doctors of personal finance based on our definition of an independent, fee-only fiduciary.

On the plus side, having the new tax office helped tremendously with the tax returns, enabling us to develop a much bigger tax practice for our clients. This is especially critical because for most people, a more sophisticated approach to tax planning can be a massive help in growing and preserving wealth. Many financial advisory firms don't want to mess with the tax return because it's a lot of work for very little profit.

We at the Financial Consulate find that it gives us the opportunity to really understand the things going on with a client, and that allows us to see quickly when that client needs implementation of a better tax strategy. As such, I consider the tax return invaluable to understand and help the client.

Tax planning isn't something that you only do when April rolls around. Most of your opportunity to save on taxes falls between January 1 and December 31. You've got to know what's going on during the year and think it out so that when you file your tax return, you're fully prepared. There is also always an opportunity to see mistakes made in prior years that can be corrected in the current year.

As I mentioned in Chapter 2, there is a big difference between tax preparation and tax planning, and that's what an advisor who acts like a doctor of personal finance focuses on with their clients.

Staffing Freedom

Another big change in 2014 occurred when Tim opted to leave the practice. He had been so crucial in helping our clients, bringing on Mike as an intern and doing television appearances representing our firm. He wanted to stay in the industry but no longer wanted to be in Maryland. Because my goal is always to help my employees find their greater calling, I was thrilled to know that the media we'd encouraged Tim to do had elevated his profile enough that it helped him secure his next position in the industry in the state of his choice. Then, as now, our motto states, "Free to come, free to go."

I truly believe that my job is to steward our employees, associates, and clients toward their destinies in life, not to hold them back. If an employee's destiny is not with the Financial Consulate, I will do what I can to help them, no matter how painful it can be to lose an employee.

Eventually, we replaced Tim, and by the end of 2018, we had recruited a total of twenty folks passionate about helping clients. One of the ways I can tell we're doing a good job in choosing the professionals who work at the Financial Consulate is by the way our clients stay with and continue to recommend us, even decades after they used our services.

I had a client back in 1981, Joan, who placed her trust in me, and I helped her with her financial planning goals surrounding the $180,000 or so she had in assets. Later in life, Joan opened a store with her friend Selma. Selma and Joan were inseparable. Even when Joan came to see me about her tax planning, Selma would be right there, waiting in the lobby.

Then one day about six years ago, Joan said Selma's husband had passed, and she had suggested that Selma meet with us to handle the estate she'd inherited. Come to find out, the estate was worth $11 million, and thankfully, with Joan's help, Selma saw that the advisors her husband had worked with were not taking her needs and expectations into account once she inherited the estate.

By that time, Joan had been my client for close to thirty years—I credit the strength of my entire team with helping me keep clients like her happy for so long.

Another client who'd been with me since my IDS days was Margaret. After I left IDS and found annuities that were better suited to her needs, I helped Margaret transfer the funds. This was a critical move because Margaret wanted those funds to help take care of her daughter, Laura.

We helped Margaret until she passed away in the mid-80s and continued to help her daughter until her death in 2022.

Having such long and intimate relationships with clients is a blessing. It can be emotionally challenging to lose a client suddenly, like Rebecca, who'd been a client of mine for over twenty-two years. She recently called to tell me that she'd been having some medical problems, but I still wasn't prepared when her cousin called me just three days later to say that Rebecca had passed.

My philosophy now is that, when a baby's being born, man reveals himself. When a person dies, God reveals himself more than anything because the death shows the emptiness and hopelessness of this world that man created. When the spirit leaves the body, it returns to where God intended it to be, to live the life that He wants us to experience.

Expecting the Unexpected

Like most of the world, we didn't expect the COVID-19 pandemic in 2020. When the lockdowns hit, it was hard to know how the market would react, and of course, every time you have a panic of some sort, there will be those people who sell out. I have relatives who even sold all their holdings in 2020, despite my advice that they just pull back a little. The same thing happened in 2008, when a small group of our clients were convinced that they had to get totally out of the market, and they couldn't stand to see it go down one more dollar.

But the fascinating thing is that the people who lose money are those who decide they can't handle it anymore and sell when the market declines. The person who loses money is not the one who says, "OK, it's down, I'm just not going to look at it and I'll see what happens a year or two from now." Instead of losing money, that person simply goes through a downturn.

So many people sell in a panic at or close to the bottom and lock in the very losses they are afraid of. And while answering the urge to sell might seem like a good way to preserve your mental health, it might harm your mental health further to sell and lock in your losses rather than watch as the market recovers without you.

Thankfully, most of our clients trusted us to do what we felt was right. In this case, as in others, it's not just about assuming that the market will always come back. While I do believe there's a good possibility that's the right answer, there can always be a scenario where the market does not recover, and you have to be cautious about that. No matter what, it's never a good choice to panic when the markets go down, even during an unprecedented event like a pandemic.

If you're retired and taking an income from your IRA, it's generally a much better plan to have some conservative assets available in the account that can carry you for two or three years so you can avoid liquidating at the wrong time.

Many people believe that a professional advisor should be able to sell at every downturn before it happens and buy back in at the bottom when it's ready to go back up. But we don't have a crystal ball and have no better ability to time the market than you do. Instead, financial management is about understanding each client's psychology, financial needs, and risk level before they start investing. This allows us to plan more conservatively for those who will endure the most psychological impact from a downturn and for those who will have the most need for their assets in the near future.

The Loss of a Breadwinner

The COVID pandemic changed the dynamic of many families, as many income-earning spouses and parents unexpectedly passed away. The death of a breadwinning spouse often comes as a surprise, which illustrates how important it is for every person to have a professional financial advisor as opposed to an insurance agent who doesn't have comprehensive knowledge, hasn't really studied or been educated about risk management, and hasn't tried to minimize the conflicts of interest.

What you really need to know is that when you die, your family will be protected. That's the key. That's what risk management's all about.

Generally speaking, life insurance isn't an investment, it's a risk management product. Yet we often see young people who make a few hundred thousand a year with a small death benefit, high premium whole life insurance policy. This insufficient coverage will have a premium around $2,000 or more, and the commission is often 100 percent or more of the first year's premium.

Yet, a term policy with four times the death benefit will have a premium of about 10 to 20 percent of the smaller policy, and a commission of a $100 or so. The average insurance agent can't make a living off that, so they convince themselves that this permanent life insurance is good for their clients.

One of the toughest decisions a surviving spouse must make after the loss of the breadwinner is whether to use the life insurance death benefit to pay off their mortgage. If we have a widow who receives only $500,000 after the loss of her husband, and they have a $300,000 mortgage, the liquidity—or available cash—from the death benefit might be better set aside than spent paying off the mortgage, especially if the widow doesn't have enough income to get an equity loan on the property after paying it off. The truth is, you don't know whether you will need a large amount of cash, and that death benefit could literally be the only time the surviving spouse has access to one.

Every situation is different, but overall, one of the biggest mistakes we see survivors make after losing the family breadwinner is overspending and justifying why they need to spend the money. Often, the overspending is simply the result of the emotional impact of the loss. It can be dangerous to have access to a large sum of money at a time when your emotional status could be driving your decision-making and you can easily fall into the trap of trying to make yourself and your children feel better by spending. Sadly, people often don't realize that this won't work until after the money's gone.

As financial advisors, we are always trying to do the right thing by our clients. Going through the loss of personal friends and family members over the years brought in a new dimension to planning. It showed me firsthand how the influence of a fee-only, credentialed, knowledgeable financial advisor fiduciary made a difference in the lives of those we help.

Of course, knowing how critical our help is to our clients makes it just that much more frustrating when a steady flow of people come in with auto and home insurance that's totally inappropriate for their net worth. Or life insurance that's totally inappropriate for where they are in life now. Or long-term care where agents use misleading fear to drive sales. The public has no idea how the whole industry, whether it's lawyers or accountants or advisors, are guiding them with all their economic biases completely in the way.

Our Firm Today

Today, the Financial Consulate is still doing what it does best—providing fee-only financial advice by educated, certified, credentialed, and experienced professionals held to a fiduciary standard. Over the last five years, I've been scaling back my administrative role, and in 2020, I turned over daily management responsibilities to Mike, giving him a well-deserved promotion to chief executive officer and president.

Mike and five others on the team have formed a guidance committee, and together they determine the direction the company will go in so that it continues to provide agile service to our customers and their heirs. We also have a group of younger professionals in their twenties who are studying for their CFP* credential and gaining experience by working with the more established planners in the firm.

Because of the knowledge and passion of our associates, we are constantly looking at new investment and financial management concepts, including products such as life settlements, private REITs, no-commission annuities, cryptocurrencies, NFTs, opportunity zone funds, and so forth. In addition, many of our clients have investigated private equity opportunities.

Altogether, I think we have built the strongest team in the company's history, and I'm constantly blown away by how phenomenal my colleagues are. I have taught each of our employees that if they focus on earning more and more money throughout the course of their career, they will be greatly disappointed come retirement. But if they come to work every day thinking about what they can do to help somebody else and focus on doing the right thing for everyone, they will be like me—enjoying their work while also making a very good living.

Earlier, I mentioned our logo was an interpretation of Dupont Circle in Washington where many embassies are located, but that is an oversimplification. While that is the inspiration behind the design, the individual elements of the logo have even more meaning behind them.

The white circle in the center of the logo represents our company's mission statement, which is **to help our clients lessen the worry and burden of money management so they can focus on the true power of life, which is relationships.** The gray inner circle represents our employees taking that mission and pushing it out toward the outer gray circle, which represents our clients. The white breaks in the circle represent our firm's openness and the fact that we are always seeking new clients and employees who are dedicated to our mission.

In my position as chairman, I am now solely focused on working with clients, tax planning, conducting webinars, hosting the radio show, and educating the public, which is why I decided to write this book. What I want, more than anything, is to continue to deliver the message that what the public really needs and really wants is a professional, fee-only financial advisor who is an experienced fiduciary with credentials and education just like a general practitioner of medicine.

I also want to make it clear that with most financial advisors out there, that is NOT what you are getting. Yet you pay as much or more for their services as you would for a professional advisory firm acting as a fiduciary.

How Our Fee-Only Planning Firm Works

When you work with us as a fee-only planner, the fees are based on the assets that we actually manage or supervise. Managed assets are those assets that we make discretionary decisions regarding. Supervised assets are those assets you manage on your own, and we oversee and can easily update your goals and act as a fail-safe to your family.

The percentage fee charged on your assets decreases at certain benchmarks, like $1 million and $5 million. Still, the more your portfolio is worth, the more we get paid. That is our economic bias. As fiduciaries, not only do we disclose conflicts of interest to clients, but any time we make a planning suggestion, we must be able to demonstrate why it is beneficial.

Right now, one client we're working with is a great example of how we make decisions based on our clients' interests, not our own. This gentleman, Eric, was with a very large Wall Street firm whose name you would recognize. That firm that was charging him about 25 percent more in fees than we are charging him. Worse, they made sure to talk Eric into decisions that were not in his best interests but that did increase the fees he pays.

One example was through the 529 plan Eric set up for his kids. In most states, there is a state-sponsored plan that may offer tax benefits, has lower management fees within the plan, and pays no commissions. Instead of suggesting that Eric invest in his state's plan that did offer tax benefits, his former advisors suggested a Virginia plan—one that paid commissions.

As fiduciaries, we have no choice but to tell a client that they should be in the plan of their state, if it's appropriate. When you consider the fact that the underlying investments in a 529 plan are not managed by the advisor, it makes no sense for them to get paid a commission or fee on the plan.

Another area where Eric was not getting tax or fiduciary advice was with his retirement planning. When we looked at his portfolio, we found that Eric had a large sum in what's called nondeductible IRAs, when it could easily have been converted into a Roth IRA to ensure tax-free, qualified distributions during retirement. To do this, we had to move his pretax traditional IRA balance to his traditional 401(k), thereby further reducing the funds we manage.

As a fiduciary and as a professional advisor, I have an absolute duty to figure out the best strategy for every client. Not only that, but I have a duty to identify those investments that shouldn't even be managed by us and guide the client to roll IRA assets into a 401(k), which also increased liability protection for Eric who, as a professional, had personal liability.

Another example would be someone turning seventy-one, still working, and holding large traditional IRA balances. By suggesting they do a direct rollover to their 401(k) plan where they work, then those assets have no required minimum distributions (RMD) the next year when they turn seventy-two. Not having to take required minimum distributions is a tremendous tax-saving opportunity.

We have been praised and ridiculed for doing the right thing for these clients. As a fiduciary, similar to a doctor of personal finance, it is the professional recommendation. (This strategy only works for a direct rollover to a 401(k) with a current employer where you are not an owner.)

Is Your Advisor Fee-Only?

If you take only one lesson away from reading this book, I hope it's this: Every single person out there who has a financial advisor should find a National Association of Personal Financial Advisor member (NAPFA), independent fee-only fiduciary advisory firm that can be like a doctor of personal financial comprehensive advice.

Here are just a few common firms that are *UNLIKELY to have* NAPFA, independent, fee-only fiduciary comprehensive advisors:

- Merrill Lynch
- Morgan Stanley
- UBS
- Wells Fargo
- Edward Jones
- Raymond James
- LPL Financial
- Ameriprise

- Lincoln Financial
- RBC
- Northwestern Mutual
- PNC Advisors

This list is not exhaustive but merely reflective of how pervasive the sales side of the financial services world is. In 1979 I worked for a company that was taken over by Ameriprise, then moved on to Raymond James from 1981 to 1995. As I mentioned earlier in the book, Raymond James did an annual trip that was all-expenses paid, but it's really the clients who paid for these trips. This realization was one of the catalysts for me to leave the company.

Brokerage firms like Raymond James still do significant sales incentives for large revenue generators, and I would not be surprised if most of the above-listed firms do sales incentives for their representatives. I would not want my doctor doing that, and you do not want your financial advisor taking sales incentives.

Tools for Financial Planning

This chapter covered the nuts and bolts of what working with a fee-only fiduciary is like and covered some of the difficult decisions that must be made after the loss of a family's breadwinner. In this, the final section of tools for planning, I want to leave you with four general tips that will help you in your overall financial planning:

- Avoiding identity theft
- Leveraging your money story
- Investors must always be optimists

Avoiding Identity Theft

Identity theft is something everyone should be seriously concerned about. When I talk about identity theft, I'm not talking about simple credit card theft, where someone gets your credit card number and makes purchases. I'm talking about someone buying your information from the dark web and using it to open accounts in your name. The number one thing you can do to protect yourself from identity theft is to freeze your credit reports. Doing so will prevent new creditors from accessing your report and issuing new credit lines and accounts.

There are three major credit reporting agencies—Experian, Equifax, and TransUnion—and there's a quirky little one out there called Innovis. Below are links to freeze each credit bureau. Having your reports frozen may cause a nuisance for you if you're applying for a new loan, changing cell service, or switching your auto insurance, so you also want to have a strategy for "thawing" them out.

Generally, to do this, you will go online to each credit bureau. Thawing can be done in minutes if you have access to your username and password. Rather than unthawing all your reports, you might ask the company you plan to apply through which credit reporting agency they use.

- www.equifax.com/personal/credit-report-services/credit-freeze/
- www.experian.com/freeze
- www.transunion.com/credit-freeze
- https://www.innovis.com/personal/securityFreeze

Another way to guard against identity theft is to put two-factor authentication on all your accounts, even if they are not financially related accounts. Email accounts, website accounts, bank and utility accounts—whenever you have the option to turn on two-factor authentication, you should.

Also you should set push notifications to text you if anything on your profile were to change or if assets are going to be sent from an account. Notifications is the last line of defense—if hackers get through to your account, you will be notified something is underway and you are not doing it.

I do not use monthly fee–based identity theft services, but I certainly would not advise a client to not pay for one. In my opinion, the above is solid protection, but to add a monthly service is another layer of protection.

Exploiting Your Money Story

In Chapter 3, I talked about how important it is to write down your experiences with money so you can analyze events that happened in your past and how they impact the way you think about money today. This narrative you create is referred to as your money story.

Not only is your money story helpful in encouraging you to change your behavior and relearn how to think about money, it's also helpful in leveraging your individual triggers to make you spend less. Allow me to explain.

Generally, there are five ways you can make a purchase: with cash, with a debit card, with a check, with an app like Venmo, or with a credit card. When you examine your money story, you may find that you are partial to using one or two methods over the others. You may find that there are one or two ways to pay that are easy and even enjoyable for you.

On the flip side, you may discover there are ways to pay for things that you feel negatively about. For example, the idea of writing a check in a grocery store might give you cold chills of dread. Or perhaps paying with cash, allowing you to see your stack of money dwindle, alarms you.

Once you determine those payment methods that are easy for you to use and elicit positive feelings, stop using them and restrict yourself to only using those methods you are negative about, because it will change the way you view the activity of spending. To illustrate how this works, let me use an example from my own life.

When I was a kid, my parents used to take us on vacation, and my father would give us each $5 to spend however we wanted. His one rule, which he was very strict about, was that we had to spend it on vacation. The urgency of needing to spend this $5 during a limited time stuck with me, and later, as an adult, I began to notice that any time I had cash in my pocket, it flowed out like water. Once I realized this, I stopped carrying cash and instead relied on my credit cards, which I used more reluctantly.

As an accountant, I get antsy when that checking account balance gets anywhere near the red. I want it to stay in the black, period. So in Quicken, I made an entry at the end of my ledger called "escrow for credit cards." Then, whenever I used my credit card, I would enter a transaction for that much in the Quicken ledger under escrow for credit cards. The more I escrow, the closer to red my checking account balance becomes, and the less likely I am to spend. An added benefit is that I know exactly what the credit card bill will be, and I already have funds set aside to pay it.

My wife, on the other hand, has an incredible regard and reverence for cash. Her father used to cash his paycheck and put the proceeds into five or six envelopes: one for gasoline, one for groceries, one for rent, and so on. He took that money out of envelopes *only* for those situations. So my wife saw cash used with reverence, and it affected her.

Earlier in the book, I told you about the difficult period my wife and I went through regarding credit card use. When she realized why she was using the credit cards and wanted to change that habit, my wife went to all cash because she wanted to use the payment form she had the most reverence for. She got rid of the payment method she was more comfortable with and had an easier time using. My stepdaughter Melania has also integrated this lesson into her own life and has told me what a remarkable difference it's made, essentially revolutionizing her spending.

If you need to control your spending, figure out which payment method you have the most reverence for and which one is easiest for you to use. Then, restrict yourself to only spending money by that method you revere. It will slow down your spending tremendously, helping you accumulate more and funnel your savings toward those things that really matter to you.

Investors Must Always Be Optimists

I mentioned a few times in this book how important it is for investors to be optimists, much like Charles Schwab and Warren Buffett are. It may seem like a throwaway comment or some way to jump on the positivity bandwagon, but being an optimist is absolutely vital for successful investors.

Imagine if someone born in 1920 was alive today, at the ripe old age of 102—let's call him Alfred. When Alfred was five years old, his rich grandfather died and gave him a portfolio worth $1,000. Alfred invested it in the stock market, but got pessimistic about the US and the markets, and decided to sell everything in 1950. He might have made some small profit, but he certainly wouldn't have done as well as his hypothetical twin brother Beau, who also inherited $1,000 from their grandfather and also invested that in the stock market.

You see, Beau was an optimist. He loved America and told everyone he could that it was the best country in the world. No matter what we faced—wars, downturns, recessions, or pandemics, Beau knew that America would figure out how to overcome any and all obstacles in its path. While Alfred's inheritance would have been long gone by now, Beau's would have grown to astronomical levels.

During Barack Obama's presidency, my liberal clients were thrilled and my conservative clients were absolutely convinced the world was coming to an end. Later, when Trump was in office, my conservative clients were absolutely convinced we were going to the moon while my liberal clients were convinced the world was coming to an end. One lesson you can consistently take from history is that politicians and political parties don't guarantee any kind of stock market performance. Whether you're facing a new president, a terrorist attack, an economic downturn, or a pandemic, don't sell everything thinking that you've got to get out now because the world's ending—because it's not. And even if it were, what good would selling do?

Ever since I first heard Charles Schwab say that an investor must always be an optimist, I've thought long and hard about it. His is one of the simplest and truest statements I've heard. It's when you get pessimistic that you make bad decisions. From optimism comes good decisions. Not greedy—optimistic.

It's just as Warren Buffett pointed out in Berkshire Hathaway's 2014 letter to shareholders:[79]

"Indeed, who has ever benefited during the past 238 years by betting against America?" [80]

---

79 For more information about these topics and more, please visit the Financial Consulate's Knowledge Center: https://financialconsulate.com/knowledge-center/

80 https://www.berkshirehathaway.com/letters/2014ltr.pdf

Conclusion

When I went into this industry over forty years ago, a financial firm hired me, sent me to Minneapolis, Minnesota, gave me two weeks of sales training, sent me back to Baltimore, and said, "You're a financial advisor. Now go out there and give financial advice." Regardless of the label they wanted to slap on me, looking back, I know that I had no idea what I was doing. If I was successful and I stayed in the industry, they were happy. And if I didn't, they couldn't care less. They expected most of us to be out of the industry by the end of the year. They simply hoped they'd get a couple of family members as clients before we left.

Believe it or not, advisors today are given as little training and support as I was. Firms still bring people in and train them in sales, focusing only on selling techniques and product knowledge. Many of these firms discourage their people from taking the CFP° class. In 2021 there were more than 260,000 personal financial advisors in the US, yet fewer than 30 percent are CFP°s.[81,82]

I believe there should be a different industry standard. I believe that if someone calls themselves a financial advisor, they should be independent, certified, educated, credentialed, experienced, and a fiduciary. At

81 oes132052.htm
82 https://safelandingfinancial.com/certified-financial-planner/

the Financial Consulate, when we bring new employees into the firm, we start them as interns. After observing them and deciding whether they have potential, we may hire them as associate financial planners.

At that point, we begin teaching them how to be a financial advisor. They sit in on meetings with clients, take the CFP° courses, then, upon passing, the CFP° board exam. After that, they continue to work under the tutelage of the senior advisor in our company for another two to four years. We then encourage a second credential to be obtained, such as a CPA, CFA, MBA, or Master's in Tax and Financial Planning.

After five years with the company, we begin to allow them to start working directly with clients. Even then, after five years, they still have senior advisors to report to. Further, we all work as a team so no one advisor has to feel like an island or like they have to know everything for every client.

This is how it is at the Financial Consulate, and it's the way it should be throughout the industry. Do you want to know that you are working with a financial advisor who didn't get their start with this much intensive training? Is that who you want handling your money, your legacy, and your future? The same way you wouldn't want a doctor who skipped medical school, neglected their residency, and didn't bother with board exams, you do not want a financial advisor who only possesses very limited tax knowledge, lacks comprehensive personal finance understanding, and has mainly been trained in sales.

I hope to see this industry change during my lifetime. I pray that I will see a time when the majority of financial advisors are true fiduciaries to their clients, rather than sales associates, and that they are trained comprehensively in all areas of personal finance, including: thorough tax knowledge, estate planning, all forms of insurance products, how to conduct real risk management, Social Security, Medicare, college planning, and anything else dealing with personal finance.

Your doctor comprehensively understands the whole body, and you should want your personal financial advisor to understand all topics of personal finance and be able to help guide you to other specialists and quality vendors.

But let's be realistic. After all this time, and all this success, the industry is not going to change itself. If consumers want financial advice from a doctor of finance, with the appropriate knowledge, certifications, and experience, they are going to have to force the industry to make the change, rather than waiting for the industry to do the right thing.

This naturally leads to the question: How can you force the financial industry to give you the kind of advisors that you are entitled to, that you deserve? How can you make the industry invest the time and money into creating doctors of personal finance who can give you unbiased, comprehensive personal financial advice that isn't locked into working directly for insurance, banks, or brokerage firms?

You can do it by changing how you choose the advisors you work with *right now*. Independent, fee-only fiduciaries can be found through the membership of the National Association of Personal Financial Advisors (NAPFA).

Throughout the book, I have given you example after example of the mistakes made by advisors with too little experience or too much bias. I've also shown you how a fee-only, credentialed, experienced, true personal financial advisor can help correct these mistakes and create tax-efficient, goal-focused plans for your future. If you've gotten the message that a true professional financial advisor—one who acts like a doctor of personal finance—is better than an advisor with only investment product knowledge and a sales focus, then show the industry you understand, and demand better.

In the beginning of this book, I clearly stated the foundation of all financial planning: **The way you think about money determines**

everything you will do *with* and *for* money. The same can be said for relationships—because the way you think about your relationships will also determine what you do with and for them. I know that the true power in life is in relationships—not in money. Your relationship with God, with your family, with your friends, neighbors, and strangers will bring you more joy and wealth than money ever will.

Relationships are powerful, but they can also be used to manipulate. A personal and professional relationship should always be free to come and free to go. A professional advisory relationship will stand behind the fiduciary standard, just as a doctor stands behind the Hippocratic oath.

The sales world knows the power of relationships and uses relationships to endear you to them. That is why entertainment has always been a major expense in financial services. It is why the industry tends to hire extroverts who know how to connect with people.

What kind of relationship do you have with your advisor? Do you get comprehensive advice? Are they trained like a doctor, and do they stand behind a fiduciary standard? Are they independent? Have they worked to minimize conflicts of interest with you?

For the fees and commissions you pay, you should get full comprehensive advice from someone educated and experienced in all areas of personal finance, not just investments. Investment diversification is very similar from advisor to advisor, so do not think anyone has something unique.

In conclusion, I ask you, "Would you identify your advisor as one who acts like a doctor of personal finance, independent of brokers, banks, and insurance companies? A fiduciary, fee-only, unwilling to take commissions and referral fees? Credentialed with at least a CFP', and experienced or at least working in a team with various degrees of experience and knowledge?

You are paying for it. Therefore, you are entitled to it.

About the Author

Drew Tignanelli is the founder and chairman of the Financial Consulate, Inc., a national wealth advisory firm. An advocate for individuals and their financial needs, Drew is passionate about facilitating financial services educational opportunities and serving as an instructor for seminars to institutions and corporations.

Drew remains highly involved in conducting Financial Physicals®, fostering new and existing client relations, engaging with clients regarding tax planning and preparation, and handling the Financial Consulate's media relations. He is a comprehensive advisor specializing in tax planning, estate planning, business owners planning, investment planning, and retirement planning. His favorite financial topic to discuss with clients is minimizing taxes.

Drew believes the tax system to be unfair to moderate and above-average income individuals, and he aims to minimize the effects that taxes have on his clients. He takes great joy in finding every legal, low-risk way to minimize a client's taxes, but he is not one for taking chances. As Drew will tell you, it was a wise man who once said, "There are only two things you cannot survive: death and a government audit."

You can find Drew on the radio or internet (WCBM.com) every Wednesday at 6:00 p.m. hosting Money, Riches & Wealth, a live show covering all areas of personal finance, airing on WCBM AM 680 Baltimore, MD (phone app: WCBM). You can also listen to the podcast version of the radio show at any time by visiting the Knowledge Center on the Financial Consulate website.

Drew earned his bachelor's degree from Towson University. He is a Certified Public Accountant (CPA), a Certified Financial Planner™ (CFP®) practitioner, a member of the National Association of Personal Financial Advisors (NAPFA), and a registered NAPFA advisor.

Outside the office, Drew enjoys golfing, fishing, and cooking. Drew is the proud stepfather to Austin and Melania, and has two fantastic in-laws, Laurie and Charles. Drew and Bev adore spending time with their six grandchildren: Kees, Guy, Ivan, George, Austin Jr., and Nicholas.

They also enjoy exploring the intricacies of wine at their home in Amelia Island, Florida. Regarding wine as more than a simple beverage, Drew appreciates its deep spiritual roots. Jesus's first recorded miracle was when he changed water to wine, and at the Last Supper, he took a glass of wine and said, "Drink of it, all of you, for this is my blood of the new covenant, which is poured out for many for the forgiveness of sins." Fascinating!

Made in the USA
Middletown, DE
03 May 2023